Kanban in 30 Days

Modern and efficient organization that delivers results

Tomas Björkholm

Jannika Björkholm

Impackt Publishing
We Mean Business

Kanban in 30 Days

First published: June 2015

Production reference: 1290615

Published by Impackt Publishing Ltd.
Livery Place
35 Livery Street
Birmingham B3 2PB, UK.

ISBN 978-1-78300-090-6

www.Impacktpub.com

Credits

Authors
Tomas Björkholm
Jannika Björkholm

Reviewer
Anna Sandell

Project Coordinator
Priyanka Goel

Content Development Editor
Sweny M. Sukumaran

Copy Editors
Utkarsha S. Kadam
Vikrant Phadke

Proofreaders
Simran Bhogal
Stephen Copestake
Paul Hindle

Cover Work
Melwyn D'sa

Production Coordinator
Melwyn D'sa

Acquisition Editor
Richard Gall

About the Authors

Tomas Björkholm works as a consultant at Crisp in Sweden. Since 2008, he has been helping companies implement and succeed with Kanban and Scrum. He is also a frequently hired speaker and has held more than 150 classes about Agile and Lean for software development. This is Tomas' second book but the first in English.

Jannika Björkholm is the team manager of a developer team, and has been working with Agile methods since 2009.

We wish to thank Anna Sandell, Johan Burén, Peter Kerschbaumer, and Mattias Skarin.

About the Reviewer

Anna Sandell lives in Sweden and has spent approximately 15 years working on leading software development projects. She is always on the lookout for better ways of visualizing the progress of development teams in order to improve their work. Agile methods such as Scrum and Kanban give her lots of inspiration in this area. Her other professional interests include organizational development and writing and proofreading texts of various kinds.

In her spare time, Anna enjoys playing curling and sewing patchwork quilts.

I would like to thank my family and my nearest colleagues who helped me in implementing enough of my ideas to keep me in a creative mood.

Contents

Chapter 6: Day 15 – First Day Running Kanban   67

Chapter 7: Days 16-29 – Improving Your Process   71

Chapter 8: Day 30 – Release Planning   83

Preface

It's just an ordinary day at work for Lisa, the project leader. Already, at the parking place outside the office she meets Ted, the marketing manager. In his normal irritating way, he asks for the project status. Lisa answers with the normal "Fine" and doesn't give any more details. After three years of working with Ted, she knows that this is just his way to start a normal conversation, the request for changed requirements. That's exactly what happens today as well, as usual.

"We met some customers yesterday and they were very clear that some changes were absolutely needed", he started.

Lisa knows there was no point in arguing.

"OK", she said, "what kind of changes are we talking about?"

"Nothing big, just some adjustments. I will pass you later today. See you later, got to run."

Before he left her he fired away the phrase she hated:

"You know, we need to be Agile."

She hated that word, "agile". She didn't know what it meant. It was just used by everybody to excuse their bad behaviour.

Lisa felt that the energy from a good night's sleep was running out of her. A good night's sleep was maybe not the right description. She was no longer able to leave her work behind at the office. Instead it followed her home, spinning around in her head and didn't give her enough peace for a good night's sleep.

She knows this was just the beginning and she was right. Even before she reached her desk, the department manager Alice grabbed her.

"Don't forget to send me the report about the delays in the project. I need it by 2:00 p.m."

Lisa felt how her stress level was increasing. When they are delayed she has to spend her time on writing reports to managers about the delay, instead of spending her time with the developers and helping them speed up.

She went to the kitchen to get a cup of coffee. She had to calm down before entering the project area. She didn't want the developers to see how stressed she felt. She totally failed. And there was no help from the developers. The more stressed she felt the more silent and vague they were. No one was able to say when they thought they would be done. They were only complaining about unclear specifications, short deadlines, and scope creep. And she didn't even dare to mention that Ted would, during the day, introduce new changes.

The frustration increased inside of her. She felt torn between managers, business people, and developers.

Is it time for Lisa to give up and quit? No it isn't! It's just time for a process that can handle changes and at the same time is transparent especially when it comes to status and consequences of a late change.

Kanban is a method that can help Lisa create a process that will improve her working day. If you recognize Lisa's situation, this book, *Kanban in 30 Days* will guide you to a better situation. It will take you through the basics of Kanban, Agile, and Lean. It will also help you reach the advanced levels, not only on a theoretical level but also on a practical level. The format of the book is a 30-day calendar that day by day gives you tools for setting up a Kanban organization that is continuously optimizing your way of working. The book will be handy even if you prefer to implement Kanban principles and practices in a different way or in another timeframe as well.

There are also a lot of tips that will be helpful for the more advanced Kanban users, such as tips about where waste can be found and eliminated and also how to better understand your context and how to improve it.

Make a note

Throughout the book, you will find that we have used different words to mean the same thing. They are as follows:

- A team, development unit, and people involved in a system refers to the people who are working together or separately on features to improve the same product
- A task, story, user story, feature, item, issue, work, or work task refers to the work the team is doing

What this book covers

Chapter 1, Days 1-2 – Understanding Kanban, Lean, and Agile, covers the principles and values for Kanban, Agile, and Lean.

Chapter 2, Days 3-5 – Getting to Know Your System, covers value stream mapping as a tool to better understand your system.

Chapter 3, Days 8-9 – Visualizing Your Process and Creating Your Initial Kanban Board, informs you how to visualize your process and create your initial Kanban board, and covers some tools to help you create your Kanban board.

Chapter 4, Days 10-11 – Setting the Limits, sets the limits and covers a game to play to get an understanding of how limits improve time to market.

Chapter 5, Day 12 – Choosing the Roles and Meetings You Need, covers examples of roles and meetings that are commonly used in organizations doing Kanban.

Chapter 6, Day 15 – First Day Running Kanban, covers an example of how the agenda for the first day could look, including planning and retrospective.

Chapter 7, Days 16-29 – Improving Your Process, covers the PDCA cycle, methods to find waste, and ways to improve your efficiency.

Chapter 8, Day 30 – Release Planning, covers how to get control over your Agile projects, how to follow up projects, and find delivery dates.

Who this book is for

This book is for those of you who want to get started with Kanban. It's practical and many parts are simplified to easily get you started. It's also for those of you who have been practicing Kanban for some time and want to get help to switch to a higher gear.

Conventions

In this book, you will find a number of styles of text that distinguish between different kinds of information. Here are some examples of these styles, and an explanation of their meaning.

For Reference
For Reference appear like this

Lists
Lists appear like this

Action Point
Action points appear like this

Make a note
Warnings or important notes appear in a box like this.

> **Tip**
> Tips and tricks appear like this.

Reader feedback

Feedback from our readers is always welcome. Let us know what you think about this book—what you liked or may have disliked. Reader feedback is important for us to develop titles that you really get the most out of.

To send us general feedback, simply send an e-mail to feedback@impacktpub.com, and mention the book title via the subject of your message.

If there is a book that you need and would like to see us publish, please send us a note via the **Submit Idea** form on https://www.impacktpub.com/#!/bookidea.

If there is a topic that you have expertise in and you are interested in either writing or contributing to a book, see our author guide on www.impacktpub.com/authors.

Customer support

Now that you are the proud owner of a Packt book, we have a number of things to help you to get the most from your purchase.

Errata

Although we have taken every care to ensure the accuracy of our content, mistakes do happen. If you find a mistake in one of our books—maybe a mistake in the text or the code—we would be grateful if you would report this to us. By doing so, you can save other readers from frustration and help us improve subsequent versions of this book. If you find any errata, please report them by visiting http://www.impacktpub.com/support, selecting your book, clicking on the **Errata submission form** link, and entering the details of your errata. Once your errata are verified, your submission will be accepted and the errata will be uploaded on our website, or added to any list of existing errata, under the Errata section of that title. Any existing errata can be viewed by selecting your title from http://www.impacktpub.com/support.

Piracy

Piracy of copyright material on the Internet is an ongoing problem across all media. At Packt, we take the protection of our copyright and licenses very seriously. If you come across any illegal copies of our works, in any form, on the Internet, please provide us with the location address or website name immediately so that we can pursue a remedy.

Please contact us at `copyright@impacktpub.com` with a link to the suspected pirated material.

We appreciate your help in protecting our authors, and our ability to bring you valuable content.

Questions

You can contact us at `questions@impacktpub.com` if you are having a problem with any aspect of the book, and we will do our best to address it.

>1

Days 1-2 – Understanding Kanban, Lean, and Agile

Kanban translates from Japanese as **sign board** or **signal card**. It was this signal card that was originally used as a mechanism by car manufacturer Toyota to help them ensure that they received the required car parts just in time. A physical card was sent to the supplier as a signal that the plant needed more of a certain part. The same card was stuck to the part when it was delivered and when the part was consumed, the card, still the same, was detached and sent to the manufacturer again as a signal for the need for more parts. Essential to this process is a rule that the number of cards stays the same. The number of cards cannot be reduced or increased without a formal decision. This mechanism ensures that the number of unused parts are kept at a level that will maximize flow and at the same time minimize manufactured but unused car parts. Car parts that have still not been attached to a car body are considered as waste.

The mechanism is also used in the Imperial Garden in Tokyo. That's where a certain David J Anderson saw the possibility to convert the ideas to software development. This is the story I heard from him: He came to the garden and a guard asked if he had a ticket. Since he didn't have a ticket he got one for free. He was a little confused about it and got even more confused when he, at the exit, was asked to give the ticket back. He later understood that the ticket was a controlling system, making sure the number of people inside the park was under a certain limit. I guess they had found out that if the number of people exceeded this number then the crowd would make people walk on the grass to pass each other and the park would be destroyed. David, who was working at Microsoft at the time, saw similar problems with software development. When people took on too much work in parallel it caused problems like bad quality and late deliveries. Together with the Kanban community, he created the Kanban method that is described in this book.

In this book we will use the definition of Kanban that is described at the Lean Kanban University (http://edu.leankanban.com/).

In this chapter, we will cover the first two days of learning Kanban, and we will learn about Kanban, Agile, Lean, and also the difference between Kanban and Scrum.

Let's begin by looking at the four foundational principles and six core practices of Kanban.

The four foundational principles of Kanban

The Kanban method is described by the following foundational principles:

> ➤ Start with what you do now
>
> ➤ Agree to pursue evolutionary change
>
> ➤ Initially, respect current roles, responsibilities, and job titles
>
> ➤ Encourage acts of leadership at all levels

The four principles make it clear that the Kanban method is not a process in itself to just put in practice, it's a method to drive improvement and it starts with the process you already have. Bullet 1 and 3 say clearly to not make any changes neither in the process nor in the roles, initially. Bullet 2 and 4 set your mind to involve everyone to take small steps of improvement that will be permanent. Kanban is not a destination, it's a direction and wherever you are, you can always apply these principles.

The six core practices of Kanban

Beside the four principles there are six core practices to follow when using Kanban; stick to these six and you will be on your way to get a streamlined Lean system that works effectively. Kanban works on a personal as well as on an organizational level and both on big and small companies.

Practice 1 – visualizing your work

The first practice is to *visualize what you are doing*. This includes both the steps in the process and what work you currently have in each step.

You can use an electronic board or a physical whiteboard. It's great to have an electronic tool but so far I haven't seen anything that beats a big whiteboard. A whiteboard, because of its size, will easily give you an overview of the status and it´s flexible; you just draw new lines and add text wherever it's needed. The whole team can stand around it, get a good understanding about a project or process, and they can update the status simultaneously. If you can get a whiteboard on wheels, you can take it with you when you are in meeting rooms. The following image shows you how your whiteboard may look, with each column signifying a step in the process and the cards indicating the work you have to do in each.

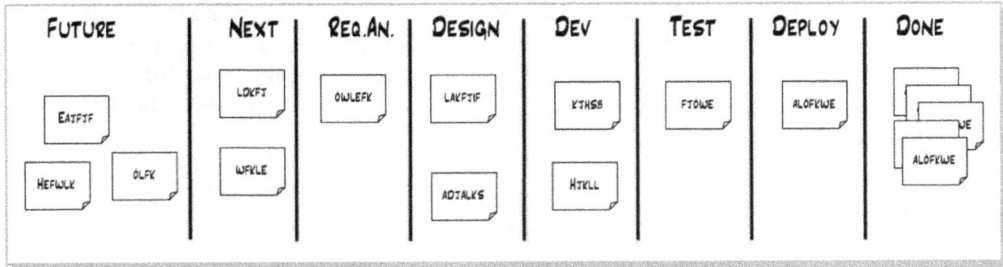

Process steps and work shown on a Kanban Board. In this example it starts with an unsorted queue for future tasks followed by the sorted queue for the tasks to undertake next. The following process steps are one each for analyzing the requirements, designing the software architecture (design), development, testing, and deployment. At the end is a column for tasks that are done.

Practice 2 – limiting work in progress

The second practice is about limiting work in progress, also called **WiP**. By setting limits, you are not allowed to bring more work in than you are able to handle. If the persons working in the earlier process step work faster than the ones in the next step, then the work stays in the column until there is available capacity in the next step and they are ready to bring it in. Because of rule 2, the earlier steps are not allowed to bring more things in than what its limit allows. This is to prevent you from building queues of half-done work inside the system. Piles of unfinished work are one of the biggest wastes according to the Lean philosophy. What are people that are working in the early steps to do if they have reached the limit and are not allowed to bring more work in? Either they do nothing or even better, they check what they can do to help the bottleneck.

The following image shows the same Kanban Board when you have added limits:

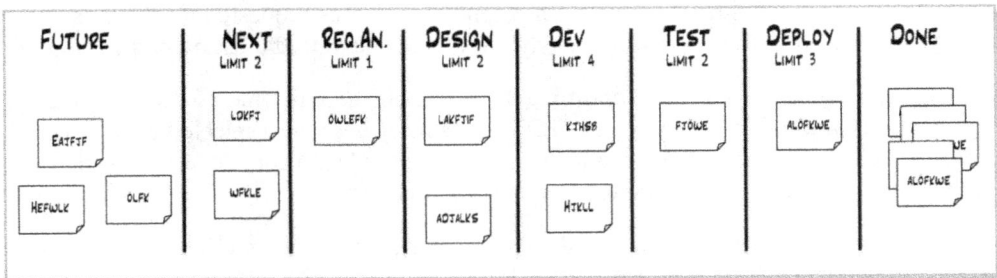

Process steps, work, and limits shown on a Kanban Board. If requirement analysts, who have a limit of 1, are done then they can't bring more work in since the next step, the design step, has reached its limit of 2. The only way for requirement analysts to get an empty slot is when designers have available slots.

In the example, you can see that the process steps **Next**, **Requirement analysis,** and **Design** have reached their limit. It might be that the **Design** step is the bottleneck and that the people working with requirement analysis are doing nothing. We don't know that by just looking at the Kanban board but we do know that they are not allowed to start working on something new.

Practice 3 – managing flow

The third practice is about improving the flow of a process so the time-to-market, also called lead-time, is decreased.

This image describes the lead-time for an item.

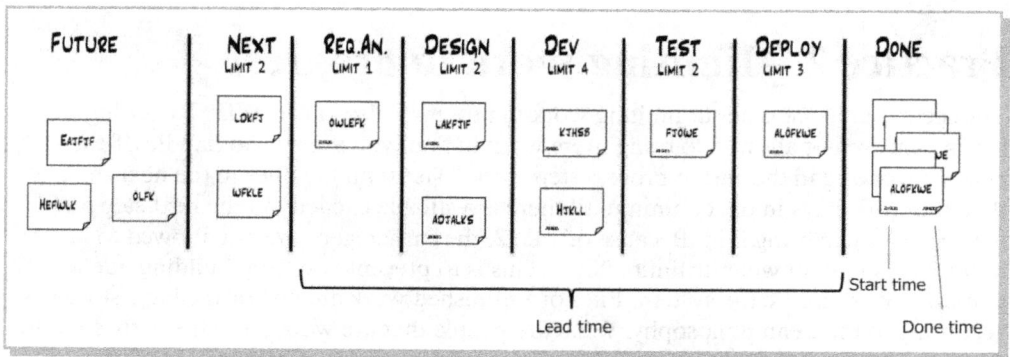

Lead-time is the time from when we start working on an item until we are done with it

The lead-time could be measured in many different ways. In the previous example, the lead-time is from when we start working on the item until we have deployed it. It would also make sense to measure the time from when the item was requested until it was deployed. In the diagram this would be when the item gets into the list named **FUTURE**.

Since the third practice tells us to optimize the lead-time, here is where we start changing organizations and the way they work. This is not simply because a selected process tells us to, but because we believe the change will decrease the lead-time. Our belief is that the organization is more willing to change when they know why.

The value of the requested product is likely to decrease over time and that's the reason for the third practice. We don´t want it to take too long a time from the request until we deploy the product.

Practice 4 – making process policies explicit

The fourth practice is about being clear about the process and the policies and principles behind it. This is to make sure everybody involved knows and follows the process and can suggest improvements of it. The reason is simply that it's very hard to discuss and improve a process unless you know what the current process is.

Practice 5 – implementing feedback loops

According to practice 3, you should measure and optimize the lead time and this will help you become successful. But wait a minute, just delivering fast is not everything; delivering the right things is also important. To know this you need to know what the customers, the end users think, and how well the product contributes to your company's revenue and wellbeing. Here is where practice number 5 comes into the picture, the need for getting feedback from people outside of your system. There is also a need for feedback loops within a system to make sure you deliver the expected functionality with the right quality. Here is where different kinds of tests come into the picture. Automated tests that run continuously are preferred since they make feedback loops shorter.

Practice 6 – improving collaboratively, evolving experimentally (using models and the scientific method)

The sixth practice is the one that makes Kanban more interesting, as well as more complicated. This practice tells us to use all theories about flow you can find and apply it to your process in order to fulfil practice number three (optimizing lead-time). These theories can be Lean, queuing theory, chaos theory, gaming theory, theory of constraints, and probably many more. This will take a while to learn, but it will be worth it in the long run. The practice also tells us to take decision of changes in consensus to make sure everyone is aligned with the decision.

Lean

Lean is a management philosophy developed at Toyota. The Kanban process with signal cards described at the beginning of the chapter is a part of Lean, but there are many other components to it as well. It is described in 14 principles, which tell us to think long-term and focus on quality and the smoothness of a process's flow. It is centered upon the understanding that cost originates from more things than machines and people. There are invisible costs that exist between people and machines. For Toyota, it is car parts that were waiting to be used. These parts not only required storage and transportation but also risked being damaged during transportation. There was also the chance that they would grow old in storage and at the end be thrown away because they were not needed anymore.

For software development, these in between costs can be found in pre-studies, design documents, and code that have not yet been released to the market. You have the cost but no value. Some of this will become valuable but some of it will be outdated before it generates any value. The Lean idea is to reduce the risk for outdated products by shortening the time to market or at least the time before you get feedback. You want to know if you are doing the right things or not and you want to take as little risk as possible.

Besides the 14 principles, Lean is a way of thinking and an attitude. It is about challenging problems, continuously improving and continuously striving for perfection. With a Lean attitude, we know that our competitors have the same problems that we have, and if we are a little better than the competitors dealing with the problems, then we are ahead of them in our competition.

When I (Tomas) was in Japan 2009 visiting Lean companies, something I repeatedly heard was "if we are not a little better next week than we are this week, we will sooner or later be out of business". When visiting European and American companies I do more often hear "we are the best". Lean companies are looking for perfection; they do not settle with just being the best for now.

In the Lean attitude, there is also a way of handling visions that are overwhelming. It is a simple way and can be described with these steps:

1. Define your vision even if it feels impossible to reach.
2. Define where you are now.
3. Define what next reachable goal in the right direction.
4. Iteratively make improvements until the goal is reached.

Steps 2 to 4 should be repeated forever, as long as the vision is still valid. If it is not, you will need to go back and find a way of redefining it.

This image shows the Lean attitude:

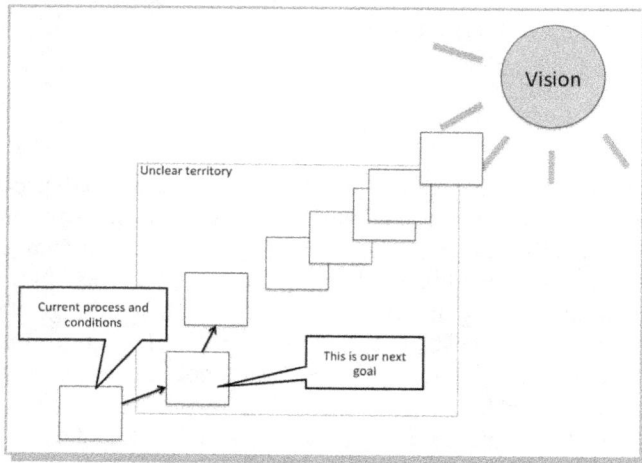

A Lean attitude is a way of taking small steps in the direction toward the vision

There is another way of looking at the way of taking small steps towards the vision. When you have employers who are very fond of Kanban, they might complain that you're not taking the big steps to the vision immediately. This thinking helps people understand that it's hard to take those big steps and that the vision might be easier to reach by taking small steps. The organization is then able to slowly, at its own pace, make changes. Those who are eager for big steps can feel calm knowing that the company is moving in the right direction.

Lean is also about ensuring that workers are encouraged and expected to continuously suggest and implement improvements in their way of working. To be able to contribute, everyone needs to get the full picture. That's why visualization is so important in Lean.

The 14 principles of Lean

Long-term philosophy:

> ➤ Base your management decisions on a long-term philosophy, even at the expense of short-term financial goals

The right process will produce the right results:

> ➤ Create continuous process flow to bring problems to the surface
> ➤ Use the "pull" system to avoid overproduction
> ➤ Level out the workload (heijunka) – work like the tortoise, not the hare
> ➤ Build a culture of stopping to fix problems to ensure quality right from the start
> ➤ Standardized tasks are the foundation for continuous improvement and employee empowerment
> ➤ Use visual control so no problems are hidden
> ➤ Use only reliable, thoroughly tested technology that serves your people and processes

Add value to the organization by developing your people and partners:

> ➤ Grow leaders who thoroughly understand the work, live the philosophy, and teach it to others
> ➤ Develop exceptional people and teams who follow your company's philosophy
> ➤ Respect your extended network of partners and suppliers by challenging them and helping them improve

Continuously solving root problems drives organizational learning:

> ➤ Go and see for yourself to thoroughly understand the situation (Genchi Genbutsu)
> ➤ Make decisions slowly by consensus, thoroughly considering all options (Nemawashi); implement decisions rapidly
> ➤ Become a learning organization through relentless reflection (Hansei) and continuous improvement (Kaizen)

Source: "The Toyota Way" by Jeffrey K Liker.

Agile

Agile, like Lean, is more of a culture than a process. Agile is defined by 4 values and 12 principles, telling what the 17 authors of the manifesto have discovered to be important when it comes to effective software development. In short, you could say it's about getting fast feedback and being technically and mentally prepared for changing direction. Some describe this in a negative tone as "you never know what you will get". We would say that it's more correct to say that we never know from the beginning what the user or customer needs so we have to use a process that makes it possible to learn and adjust along the way. Agile is a way of minimizing risk, the risk that the customers do no longer want what we originally thought they wanted.

When talking about risk handling, the risk of delivering the wrong product or feature is one of the more important. When starting a project, we can guess what the customers need, but it's only when the customer starts using the output of the project that we know for sure if we delivered a high value product or not. To make it even more complicated, the right product could quickly become the wrong one when time passes since customers' needs and expectations change quickly. To minimize the risk of building the wrong things, Lean and Agile values quick feedback by getting features in a testable or sellable state as quick as possible. Lean and Agile values small releases often instead of big bang releases. They do also suggest that you optimize on flow instead of resources.

Manifesto for Agile Software Development

We are uncovering better ways of developing software by doing it and helping others do it. Through this work we have come to value:

> Individuals and interactions over processes and tools
> Working software over comprehensive documentation
> Customer collaboration over contract negotiation
> Responding to change over following a plan

That is, while there is value in the items on the right, we value the items on the left more.

Source: http://agilemanifesto.org/

Principles behind the Agile Manifesto

Our highest priority is to satisfy the customer through early and continuous delivery of valuable software.

Welcome changing requirements, even late in development. Agile processes harness change for the customer's competitive advantage.

Deliver working software frequently, from a couple of weeks to a couple of months, with a preference to the shorter timescale.

Business people and developers must work together daily throughout the project.

Build projects around motivated individuals. Give them the environment and support they need, and trust them to get the job done.

The most efficient and effective method of conveying information to and within a development team is face-to-face conversation.

Working software is the primary measure of progress.

Agile processes promote sustainable development. The sponsors, developers, and users should be able to maintain a constant pace indefinitely.

Continuous attention to technical excellence and good design enhances agility.

Simplicity—the art of maximizing the amount of work not done—is essential.

The best architectures, requirements, and designs emerge from self-organizing teams.

At regular intervals, the team reflects on how to become more effective, then tunes and adjusts its behavior accordingly.

Source: `http://agilemanifesto.org/`

Self-organization

There is one more important thing about Lean and Agile: the view on decision-making. Many organizations are based on the assumption that employees should be divided into thinkers (managers) and doers (workers). This comes from Frederick Winslow Taylor who was one of the first management consultants. We think Taylor was right when he divided people between thinkers and doers just because at the time, around 1900, when he was active, there was a huge difference in education between managers and workers. His idea was that the educated should tell the uneducated what kind of products they should build and how to build them. This was a great way to get uneducated people productive in advanced industries. Today we usually don't have this difference in education. Instead, we have a lot of well-educated people in our organizations. In today's world, Taylor's ideas are wrong. To not use all the intelligence of our employees is waste.

We need all the intelligence at our disposal to collect and analyze the feedback we get by quickly getting to market and to find out how we can best improve the product. Unfortunately, a lot of managers are trained in the Taylor way of thinking. They serve the developers their working tasks in a requirement document and a design document and then they just want them to deliver the required things according to a plan. That way of working is likely to foster developers to value compliance over engagement and innovation.

If you tell people exactly what to do and how to do it, you don't give them much room to think themselves. If you instead give them goals and ask them to find the way and solve their problems themselves, you will see more energy and get far more engagement from them.

This following diagram is about fast feedback and reacting to it:

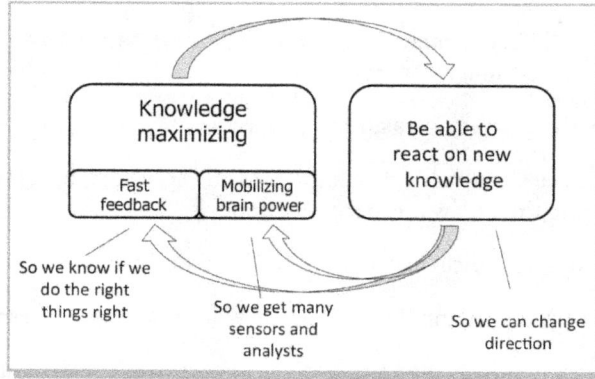

Agile and Lean is about getting fast feedback, being able to react to known knowledge and to wake up the employee's engagement.

To cultivate a culture of self-organization, managers need to build an environment where people:

> Are very aware of goals.

> Are exposed to well-visualized information of how well they are doing.

> Know they are allowed to experiment with their process. They own the process within some well-defined limits.

How to choose between Scrum and Kanban

Scrum is, like Kanban, a process framework, which applies the values and principles of Agile and Lean. In order to compare them, here is a one-minute description of Scrum.

In Scrum it is prescribed that you should have a cross-functional team, that is, a team with all competences needed to develop a whole feature. There should be a Scrum Master who is the master of the Scrum framework with the mission to make sure the team's process works well, is effective and is according to Scrum. There is also a Product Owner who knows the vision of the product, communicates with the stakeholders, and makes sure the team knows what is the right thing to be working on and in which priority.

The following diagram shows people involved in a scrum:

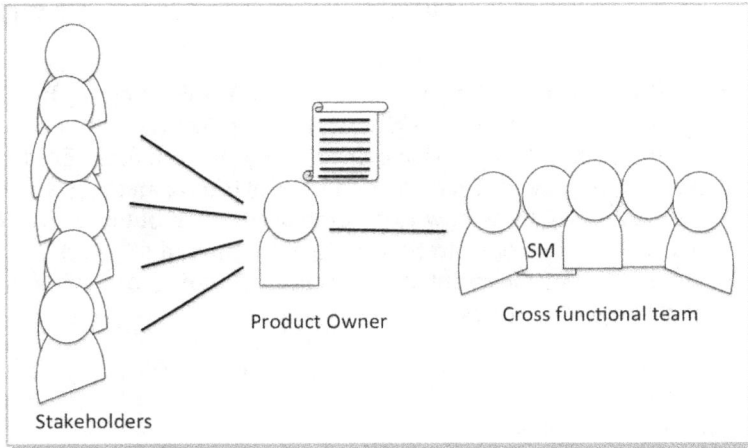

Scrum prescribes that you have a Product Owner who collects and prioritizes work to be done from the stakeholders.

In Scrum you work in iteration or Sprints of usually 1-4 weeks. Each Sprint starts with the planning of work for the Sprint and ends with a releasable increment of features. Hopefully the plan remains unchanged all through the Sprint.

Kanban has fewer rules. For instance, there is nothing about roles or about working in iterations. Kanban is more focused on continuous flow, visualizing the work and optimizing the time between ideas and runnable features.

This image shows the difference between Scrum and Kanban flow. You can easily see whether a Scrum team is at the beginning or at the end of a sprint.

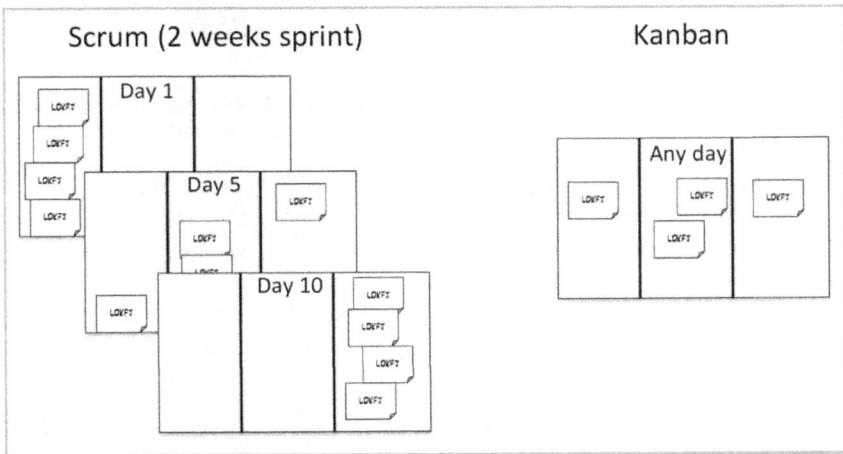

In Scrum you work in iterations called Sprints. In Kanban there is more of a constant flow

So which one, Scrum or Kanban, is the best?

That depends on the circumstances; let us tell you a story from our past to explain what we mean by that.

Some years ago, I (Tomas) was working in a team that was doing Scrum. It worked well until we got to a point where we were about to develop support for new equipment. We had a deadline coming up but the purchasing department had not been able to choose the supplier of the new equipment. I remember a print planning meeting where item after item was refused, as we didn't know how to develop drivers without knowing the supplier (items can also be called user stories). In Scrum we are supposed to give a forecast of what we would release at the end of the sprint after the sprint planning, and without knowing the supplier we couldn't give a forecast.

I suggested that we should try Kanban because it can handle just-in-time planning. We changed method and managed to get to know the supplier in the last seconds and luckily we were done in time. Kanban rocked.

The project we started after this was one of those where you think "it should work just like it did before but with the new hardware". The problem was that no one knew how it used to work. We solved it by testing the system with the new hardware one step at the time and fixed problems whenever they occurred. Again, we had a tight deadline but we made it. This made me think that Kanban really rocked.

After the second project we didn't have so much to do but fixing allot of less important small issues. Then I observed that the energy within the team was going down drastically and that even small things took time. I realized that without a goal, Kanban doesn't work very well. Scrum, on the other hand, has a built-in goal every sprint thanks to the forecast made as the output of the sprint planning. Even though the result of the planning should be considered as a forecast and not a commitment, most teams try a little bit harder just to make the forecast come true. By changing back to Scrum, we got the energy back to a high level again.

To summarize, Kanban works great with uncertainties but needs a goal while Scrum needs to have enough certainty to be able to plan a few weeks ahead.

Kanban does also have an advantage against Scrum when it comes to surviving organizational reluctance to changes. Kanban does not oblige you to change so much in the early stages of its implementation. It doesn't force you to change your organization nor your way of working, but instead provides a framework to make your organization work more effectively and efficiently. Indeed, you may well implement larger changes later, but if you do that it is because the flaws in your current organization or process have been made obvious by using Kanban.

Our advice is to not get too religious about the difference between Scrum and Kanban. Most Kanban teams we have seen have a Scrum Master, but they call it something else. It also common to have a Product Owner, meetings like Daily Standup, demo and Retrospective, and terms like "backlog" and "impediments". All this is borrowed from Scrum. Actually, there is no rule or practice in Kanban stopping you from working in iterations just like in Scrum. At least as long as working in iterations improves your flow.

Summary

In this chapter we discovered that Kanban prescribes an evolutional process change originating from your current context. We went through the six practices of Kanban in detail:

1. Visualize your process and your current status.

2. Limit how much work you have started so that you don't build queues within your system.

3. Improve your flow to decrease the time it takes from when work is started until it's finished.

4. Make process policies explicit so everybody can participate in improving them.

5. Implement feedback loops to make sure we continuously learn and implement improvements on both a local and organizational level.

6. Use known theories such as Lean, Agile, queuing theory, gaming theory, chaos theory, and theory of constraints to collaboratively and experimentally improve your flow.

We also covered Lean, which is described in 14 principles, which tell us to think long-term and focus on quality and have a continuous process flow.

We also described that Agile is about getting short feedback, and being able to technically and mentally change and mobilize brainpower. The latter does also show that Agile is a culture where respecting people, trust, and self-organization are important parts. That is an important step away from the traditional ideas about dividing people into thinkers (managers) and doers (developers).

Finally, we showed you the difference between Kanban and Scrum and discovered that the main difference was that Scrum prescribes roles, meetings, and artifacts, while Kanban is only focused on improving flow. They can also be combined. Whichever one is best depends on the situation.

In the next chapter, we will see how to get to know your process as the first step to set up your Kanban system, and how to make a value stream mapping. The chapter will give you a good foundation when you later on take steps to improve your effectiveness.

>2

Days 3-5 – Getting to Know Your System

After spending time acquainting yourself with the key theories behind Kanban, you now need to build on this knowledge with a team of colleagues that will be important to the implementation of the methodology. The aim is to understand your system in as much detail as possible so you'll have a good start when building your Kanban board that will really help you to visualize your process and also help you improve it to get even more value out of your work.

As you may have noticed, we have frequently referred to the phrase "your system". Your system is everything and everyone that is involved in your process of satisfying your customers.

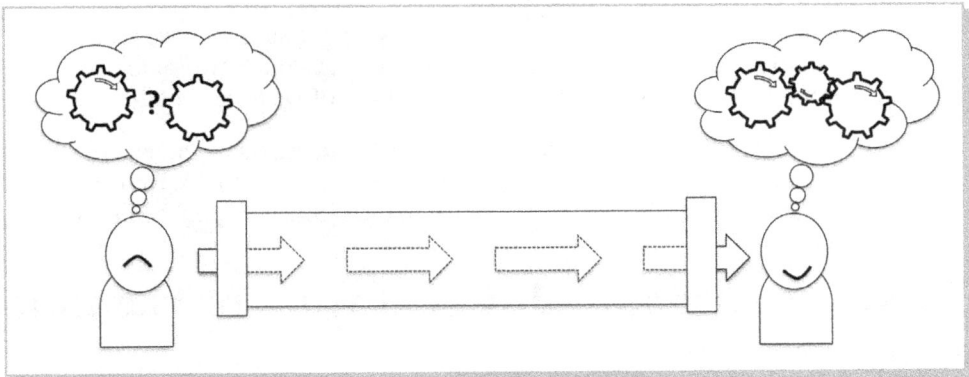

Your system is everything that happens between when your customer has a need until you have fulfilled the need. In the picture, the system is symbolized with a pipe.

It's the employees, your partners, your support systems, your organization, and your routines. The idea behind "system-thinking" is that the result depends on how all this works together.

If something goes wrong, the usual reason is not a human error, but that something is broken in the system; we need to find the fault or defect and fix it to become better. The better our system becomes, the better we fulfil our customers' expectations.

To understand your system, you need to start by answering the following questions:

1. From where do you get ideas/requests for new features or changes of existing features?

2. How is the process of delivering features, from the idea until it's implemented and delivered?

3. What makes your customers happy?

Let's take the questions one by one and start with:

Where do you get ideas/requests for new features or changes of existing functionality?

To get to the heart of this question, there are a number of other questions you can ask to help you investigate this thoroughly:

➤   Are the requests coming from one source, a few sources, or from many sources?

➤   Are the requests internal, external, or a mix?

➤   Are some sources more prioritized than others?

➤   How often do they ask for your attention?

➤   Are there any contracts stating a maximum time before answering or completing?

Answers to these questions will be important later on to make sure we have an efficient system. A system that delivers services or products to one customer two times a month will look different from a system that delivers to hundreds of customers daily.

When we know where our requests come from, we need to figure out what happens before the request has been taken care of and our customers are happy. To do this, you can use a tool called **value stream mapping**. More about that in the section *Mapping the process*.

Classes of services – different ways of handling feature requests

Usually, the feature requests coming in are of different value and urgency. Some need to be done immediately and some can wait. At this stage, it's only important to realize that different feature requests have different value and different needs for how to be treated.

There are many factors that will dictate how you respond and react to new feature requests:

> ➤ Urgency, which could be set depending on cost of delay, that is, how much it costs or how much you lose by waiting to complete the request
> ➤ Who requests the change
> ➤ Size of the request
> ➤ Whether this request is stopping something else

Consequently, according to the nature of the request, the action you take in response will be different. Some examples of how your action may be different include:

> ➤ Maximum time before responding
> ➤ Way of responding
> ➤ Way of documenting
> ➤ Way of following up

Every response requires a different type of service. This is not only because you need to pay attention to the nature of the requests, but also because a certain flexibility and adaptability is essential for your own personal and organizational workflow. Since this touches on something called **classes of services**, it's worth taking some time to look at this in more detail...

Classes of services is a way of setting a contract for how to handle issues that have close to the same need of service. A typical setup is to use these three classes, which primarily divides the request on their urgency:

> ➤ Expedite for the most urgent
> ➤ Intangible for the least urgent
> ➤ Standard for any others

In the expedite class, we might find issues that will cost the company huge amounts of money if not fixed within a certain time. It could be things that need to be done for a marketing campaign or something that's bad for the company's reputation unless it's quickly fixed. These high priority things need to be handled with another service than the issues with lower impact.

Among the issues in the intangible class, we find things that could wait some time. It could be upgrading to a new version of the development environment, improving software architecture, or fixing old bugs. They are important, but the impact for waiting another week to fix them is lower than for the other classes. Sometimes issues within the intangible class are upgraded to expedite if they have waited too long. An example is a legal issue that has a deadline far in the future. It will be in intangible class until the deadline comes close.

Mapping the process

Mapping the process that is already in place is essential if you are going to properly understand it. In Kanban terminology, a map of how your system and processes work is called a **value stream map**. As well as helping you to understand your current system, it will, more importantly, be a key step in helping you to improve your process (this will be explored in more detail in *Chapter 8, Day 30: Release Planning*). The following exercises describe a way to iterate over your process and extract one piece of information at a time.

Exercise I – draw the process steps

Decide on a typical case, feature, or issue from the "standard" service class for which you want to make a value stream map. To begin, set the coordinates between which the entire process will unfold, that is, the start and the end. At the beginning you have a customer with a need (this could be a simple problem, a missed opportunity, or even an idea); indicate this on your 'map' with a sad face so you are clear about where you are starting from. At the end of the process, you should (in theory at least) have a happy customer – indicate this with a happy face so you are clear precisely where you are going.

That's the easy bit; you now need to find the process steps between the start and the end. To do this, you firstly need to define each step. This may sound complicated, but in actual fact this is really about working out who does what, in terms of specific tasks, to fulfil an overarching goal.

One way of doing this is to view a request as a baton in a relay race. Who carries it—is responsible for it—at each step in the process? The best way of finding this out is simply through communication. If you are taking charge of the Kanban implementation, it is crucial that you get a sense of what people handle at any given moment in the handling of a request, so interviewing the team to get this understanding is a great way to do this. The dialogue would simply go like this:

> ➤ **Interviewer (I):** "What if (name of a customer) comes up with an idea they want us to develop. Whom within our company should they contact?"
>
> ➤ **Workshop member (WM):** "They will then go to George, their key account manager."
>
> ➤ **I:** "Okay, what will George do with the request?"
>
> ➤ **WM:** "He will give it to Lisa who will take it with the change control board who decide whether it's a good idea to do this or not."
>
> ➤ **I:** "So if CCB considers this idea to be good, what will happen then?"

Indeed, this workflow chain may already be perceivable, and it might happen intuitively throughout the team. However, by encouraging this kind of dialogue, you can be sure that everyone is on the same page, and that ownership of certain steps is in the right place. Even at this very early stage, having this conversation with others is a useful way of beginning to look at how the process can be improved as it encourages the team to reflect on their own role within the process while giving everyone a chance to see in an almost holistic manner how this fits together.

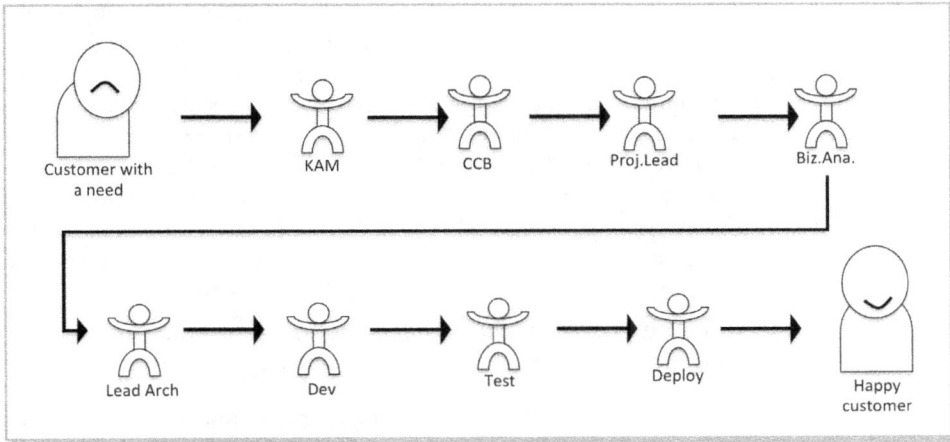

A typical value stream map after exercise 1, where only the process steps have been noted.

In this example, the customer contacts the key account manager (KAM) who takes the customer's idea to a change control board (CCB). If the idea is accepted, a project leader (PL) gives the idea to a business analyst who writes the specifications, which is handed over to a lead architect. Further down the process, the developers and the testers develop the new feature before it's deployed.

Exercise II – find the time spent on each process step

You should now know the steps in your process. The next exercise in mapping your process is to find out how much time is taken at each step in the process. Do it like this:

1. Draw triangles, symbolizing queues between each step:

    ➢   Sometimes the queue between two steps is empty (meaning the movement between the two steps is practically instantaneous and takes no time to pass).

2. Find elapsed time. For each queue, decide for how long the request on average will be waiting in the queue. Write those under the queue-triangle (see next picture). Here come some examples of how waiting time is calculated for some different scenarios:

    ➢ If someone checks a mailbox once a week, the average waiting time will be half a week.

    ➢ If a company who are working with a one-year release plan, on December 1, takes the decision for the content of the upcoming year's four releases, where the development for the releases starts in Jan, Apr, Jul, and Oct, the average waiting time until the start of a certain case will be 5.5 months. This means the waiting time before starting development for the first release will be one month (Dec -> Jan), the next releases will have a waiting time of four months (Dec -> Apr), and the sequential releases will have seven and ten months. On average, that will be 5.5 months of waiting ((1+4+7+10)/4=5.5). We know it's not very Agile to make release plans for a whole year, but since one-year release plans are still common, we wanted to give help with this example.

    ➢ If a request is put in a queue with 6 items and the average time for completion of each item is 2 weeks, the waiting time will be 12 weeks.

3. Look at every step. How long does it take for an average request to pass the step? Write those figures in the square under the step.

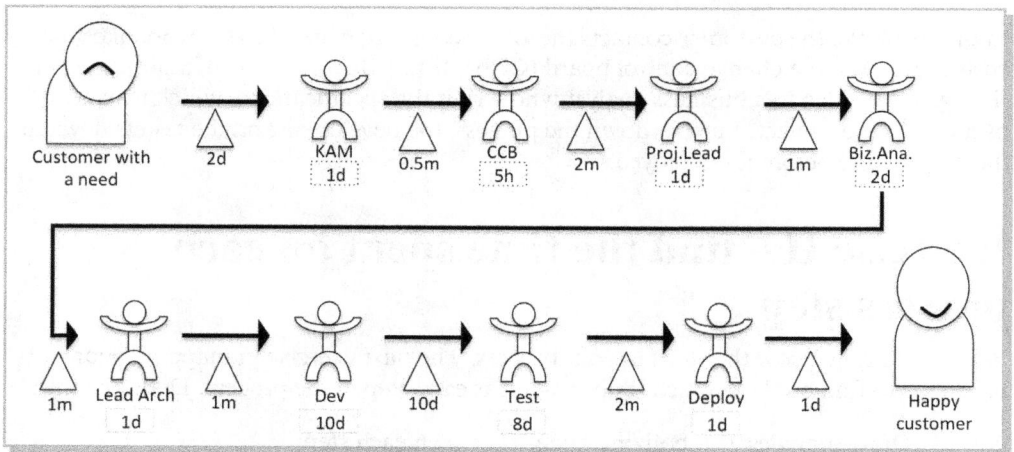

A typical value stream map including times spent for a feature from start to finish.

4. Find value adding time. Again, look at each step. If this request were the only thing handled at this step and you could work with it without interruptions, how long would it take then? Write this figure above the step. This might be the same figure as we wrote under the step. If they work with many things in parallel, have dependencies to other teams, or need to look for answers outside the team, this figure will be lower.

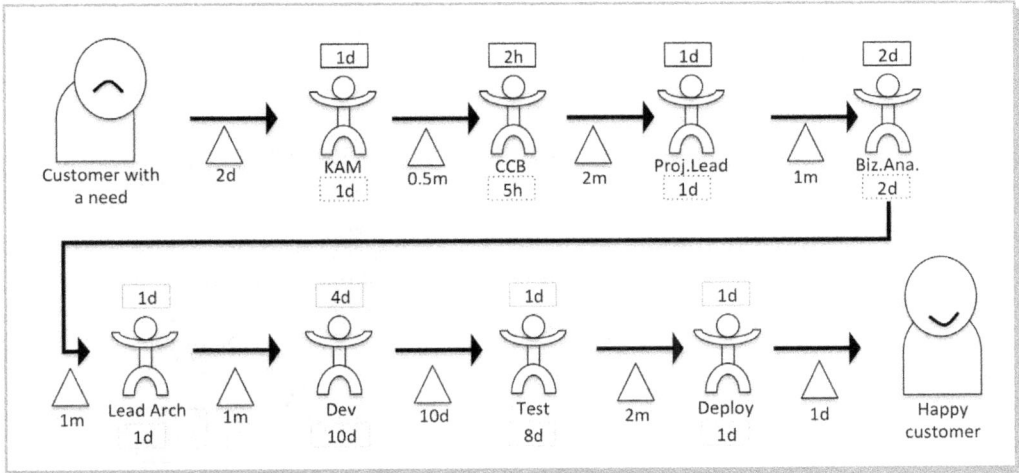

Value stream map including time for doing the work as well as waiting time

This is how extensive your map needs to be to be able to start with Kanban. In *Chapter 8, Day 30: Release Planning*, we will return to the value stream map tool to get a feeling of how well your system is doing and get hints for how we can improve it.

At this stage, the figures in the value stream map are there to help you recognize whether you need a column for the waiting time or not. It also gives you a hint of how much of a problem you have with multitasking.

What makes your customer happy?

Before you start building a board that will help you improve value outcome for your customer, you need to know exactly what your customer values.

A further workshop with the relevant members of your team should be used to try and tackle this question. Prepare the workshop by drawing a happy and a sad customer on the white board. Get your colleagues together again and start writing notes to find out what your customers value. Here are some of the most obvious examples of what your customer is likely to value – it is worth considering all of these, but also take time to work out what is likely to be the top priority:

➤ Price
➤ Service
➤ Predictability
➤ Flexibility
➤ Quick response
➤ Professional behavior
➤ Good relevant knowledge

> ➤ Honesty
> ➤ Collaboration
> ➤ Compliance

You should also ask the question of what makes your customer sad, irritated, or dissatisfied.

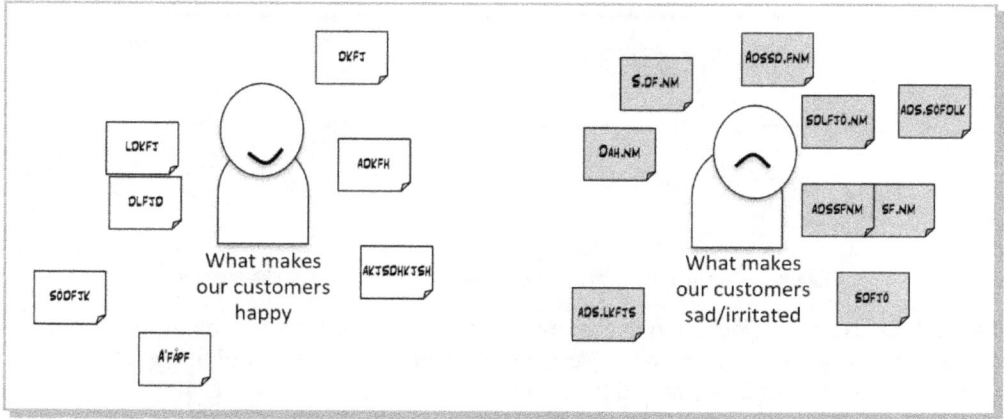

Have a workshop to find out what makes the customer happy and what does not

As always, when having workshops, making it a little bit less formal can help creativity. You could for instance ask the following question:

If the customer asks you to jump, what is your answer?

1. Okay
2. How high?
3. How much will you pay me?
4. Why?
5. Wouldn't it be better if I sing?

In a corresponding manner, you can ask the people at the Kanban workshop, "Why might a customer leave us for another supplier, write a bad comment on social media, or even sue us?"

The customers are usually not a homogeneous group. What different kind of customers do you have? How can you group them? The question of what satisfies and what dissatisfies your customer needs to be answered for each group.

Having a workshop is just a start. To really understand the customers, you need to continue the dialog and also observe their behavior. People in common are not consistent. They may answer something in an interview or at a workshop but act differently. Remember, according to the Agile values, you should work closely with your customer and be prepared for changes. This tells you to continuously have dialogs with your customers to understand what they value and what they dislike, and change your process accordingly.

More things to do to better understand your customer are as follows:

➤ See the complainers as a source of knowledge. They want to tell you something, and when they are satisfied, you know you have improved.

➤ Interview the customers that have left you, not to convince them to come back, but to understand why they are leaving.

➤ Recruit persons with a history of being your customer.

➤ Meet customers, not to sell, but to understand their daily life and what problems they are facing.

The more you know about what your customers value, the better you are able to satisfy them and the better you can form the visualization that is your Kanban board. Lean and Kanban are very much about visualizing since they help you see possibilities for improvements. They also help drive change because people are more willing to change what they can easily see as a problem.

By now you should have a good understanding of your system. That's all you need to take the next step and create your initial Kanban board, and that is what the next chapter is about.

Summary

In this chapter, we have discussed how to get a greater understanding of your system and your processes. This is an integral step in the implementation of Kanban as it will provide a foundation for you as you look to improve and refine those processes. Without an in depth understanding and appreciation of what already exists, it is extremely difficult to get the most out of Kanban.

While this process can be complex, and may sometimes take longer than the time allocated here, breaking it down into three key questions makes this process much easier:

➤ Where do ideas come from?

➤ What and how does the process work?

➤ What makes customers happy?

As you might have already noticed, these three questions all correspond to different stages in the process – the beginning, the middle, and the end. Each of these elements could be different in any process, so understanding what these might be and how they intersect is crucial.

We also went through how to draw the first part of a value stream map to get a good understanding of our process and to explore which process steps and which waiting steps consume time. In the following diagram, you see examples of two process steps and the type of information that is included in a value stream map:

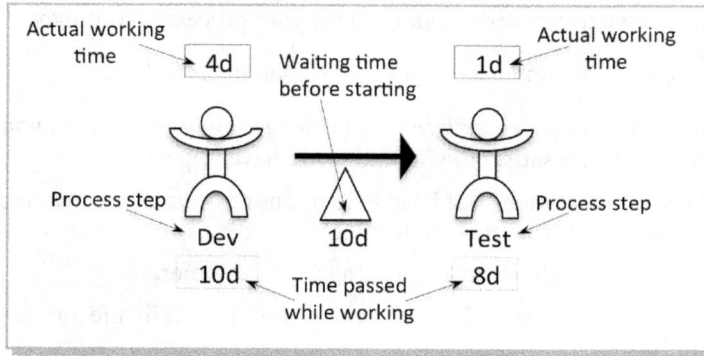

In the next chapter, you will learn how to create your Kanban board. Now you have a good understanding of how your system works, you are now ready to begin integrating your current processes with Kanban methodology. Kanban boards will look different according to the specific context in which they are used, so we will look at how to create a Kanban board that fits your needs.

> 3

Days 8-9 – Visualizing Your Process and Creating Your Initial Kanban Board

After a well-earned weekend, it's time to put the knowledge you got last week together and create your first Kanban board.

Information dimensions

Our recommendation is not to jump immediately into creating a Kanban board that looks just like the ones you have seen somewhere else. If so, all the work done last week will be wasted. Instead, take the results from your workshops and write down a list of things you think will be important to visualize and have easy access to. Let's call them "information dimensions". Examples of information dimensions are as follows:

- ➤ Status
- ➤ Priority
- ➤ Classes of service
- ➤ What to do
- ➤ Who's working on it
- ➤ Customer/origin
- ➤ Request owner
- ➤ When is it expected to be done
- ➤ Estimated size
- ➤ Test environment

What information should be shown is very context-dependent. Please take some time to figure out what kind of information is important to visualize for you.

Visualization dimensions

When you have your list of information dimensions it's time to do another list of "visualization dimensions". Hopefully you can see that your Kanban board is becoming much more layered and, indeed, multidimensional. Yes, it is becoming more complex, but with effective visualization, the increased complexity will be helpful rather than a hindrance.

Here are some examples of visualization dimensions and their benefits and drawbacks:

> ➤ Rows
>
> ➤ Columns
>
> ➤ Text
>
> ➤ Note color
>
> ➤ Pictures
>
> ➤ Magnets with text or pictures
>
> ➤ Size of notes

Of course, you may find your own way of visualizing the various elements required; the important thing is to find a way that works for you and your team.

Characteristics of visualization dimensions

The next step is to combine information with visualization dimensions. But first you should examine the different characteristics of these visualization dimensions just so you know you are using the right visualization dimension for the right information.

Following are the characteristics of some common visualization dimensions:

> ➤ **Rows**: It's easy to change row but they are limited to the space you have on your wall. Rows are very visual.
>
> ➤ **Columns**: The same as for rows.
>
> ➤ **Text**: Almost no limitations when it comes to variation but hard to change and not very visual.
>
> ➤ **Note color**: Hard to change and limited to the number of note colors that you have. The visibility is good.
>
> ➤ **Pictures**: Same as for text but a little more visible.
>
> ➤ **Magnets with text or pictures**: Flexible in how it looks, easy to move, and somewhat visual.
>
> ➤ **Note size**: The same as for note color.

Matching information and visualization dimensions

The purpose of stating the characteristics is to make sure we use the best match between the information and the visualizer. For instance, it's not a good idea to use note size to show status since the status is changing very often and note size is hard to change. If you have hundreds of customers we wouldn't recommend that you use rows to visualize them. Text is probably a better choice. On the other hand, if you have just a handful of customers, using rows to visualize which customer the work comes from is great. If you're interested to see which customer is giving you the most work the color of the note is great since it's very visual when you have a board full of notes.

Prioritizing information dimensions

The next step in building a Kanban board is to decide which information is the most important to visualize on the board. Put the information in this order:

1. Classes of service (read *Chapter 2, Days 3-5 – Getting to Know Your System* to Get a Good Understanding)
2. Status
3. Priority
4. Customer/origin
5. What to do
6. Who's working on it
7. Request owner
8. When is it expected to be done
9. Estimated size
10. Test environment
11. Type of work

Go from the top and choose the best visualization dimension that fulfils the information's characteristic. In the previous example, classes of services is the most prioritized. Since an issue can change class—something that is unimportant in August might be very important in October—you can't use the visualizers such as sizes and colors, which are hard to change.

In this case rows seem to be a good candidate since rows are a good visualizer and can be easy to change.

The second most important information dimension is status. Status is often changed so, again, colors and note sizes are not recommended. Instead, columns will fulfill our needs much better.

The third most important is priority. Since we use rows and columns this could be solved with the principle that you work the classes (rows) one by one. If the statuses (columns) are ordered so the closest to done is to the right the policy could be to work with the issues from the right. If there is more than one issue in a cell you should then work with the one positioned most to the right. The fourth-highest prioritized information dimension is origin. That is from which customer or project the work comes from. If you have fewer customers than you have note colors, then note color is a good choice for showing origin. If you have more customers than note colors maybe it makes good sense to cluster the customers in a way so that note colors could be used anyway.

Continue down your list of dimensions, matching them with the best available visualizer.

The following figure shows how you can map what you want to show with the visualization dimensions on the board:

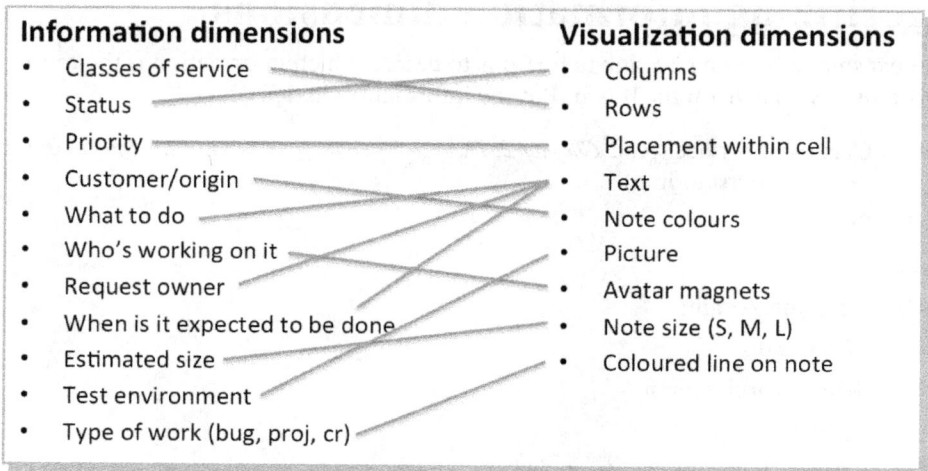

Information dimensions	Visualization dimensions
• Classes of service	• Columns
• Status	• Rows
• Priority	• Placement within cell
• Customer/origin	• Text
• What to do	• Note colours
• Who's working on it	• Picture
• Request owner	• Avatar magnets
• When is it expected to be done	• Note size (S, M, L)
• Estimated size	• Coloured line on note
• Test environment	
• Type of work (bug, proj, cr)	

For the mappings shown in the previous figure the board could look like this:

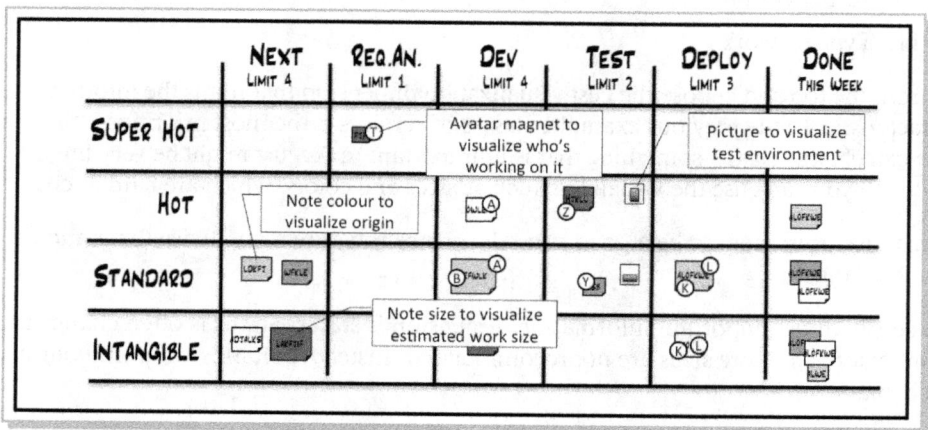

Our example Kanban board after matching information and visualization dimensions.

As you can see in the previous figure, the board has the statuses as columns and different classes of services as rows. The notes have different colors to show origin and different sizes to show the estimated size of work. Pictures of test environments show which test environment is used for certain work. This can be useful if the team is doing maintenance and projects at the same time.

Magnets with avatars show who is working with what. In the following diagram, Avatars are shown as circled capital letters. By limiting the number of avatars for each person we are at the same time making sure people are not working on too many things at the time. This will reduce the risk for time-consuming task switching and increase capacity and quality. You will now have both a system for making sure the team is not taking on too much work and making sure team members are not doing it either.

Visualizing different statuses

When deciding which statuses to show you should go back to the value stream map we talked about in *Chapter 2, Days 3-5 – Getting to Know Your System.* Do you need to visualize the steps where work is done or the queues between or both?

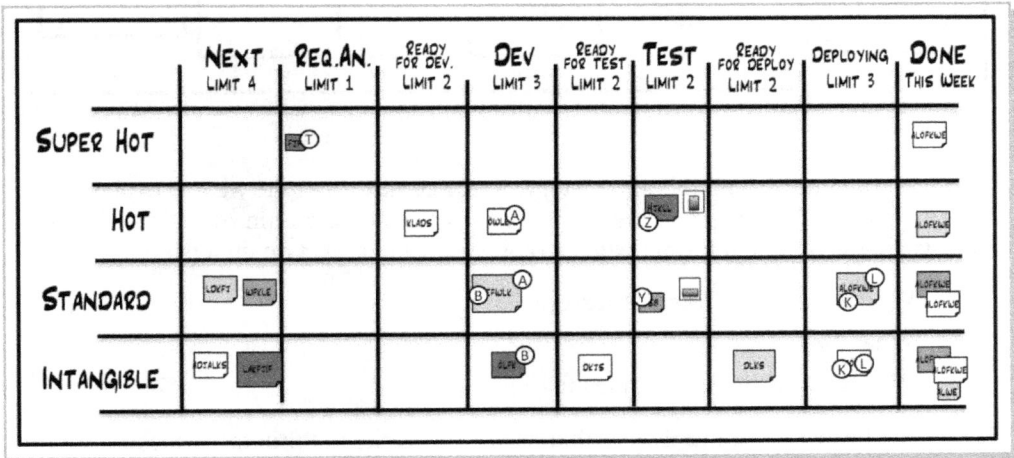

A Kanban board with both work steps and queues as statuses

The usual reason for showing a "ready for" column is when considerable time is normally consumed between the steps, that is, when something is developed but the testers aren't ready to take the case yet. If deploying is just about pressing a button or you deploy a lot of work at the same time, even if it takes some hours, there is probably no reason to have a status for that. Don't forget to have limits on queues as well as on the steps. The limits on the steps are there to make sure you are not content switching while the limits on queues are there to make sure you are not buffering up work within your system. We will explain this in more detail in *Chapter 4, Days 10-11 – Setting the Limits.*

Kanban board with stories and tasks

In the previous example we assumed there was only some work to be done within a couple of days. Here is an example of where there is more work that needs to be broken down into tasks. As you can see in the following figure, the story in the first row is divided into 5 different tasks so it will be easier to handle:

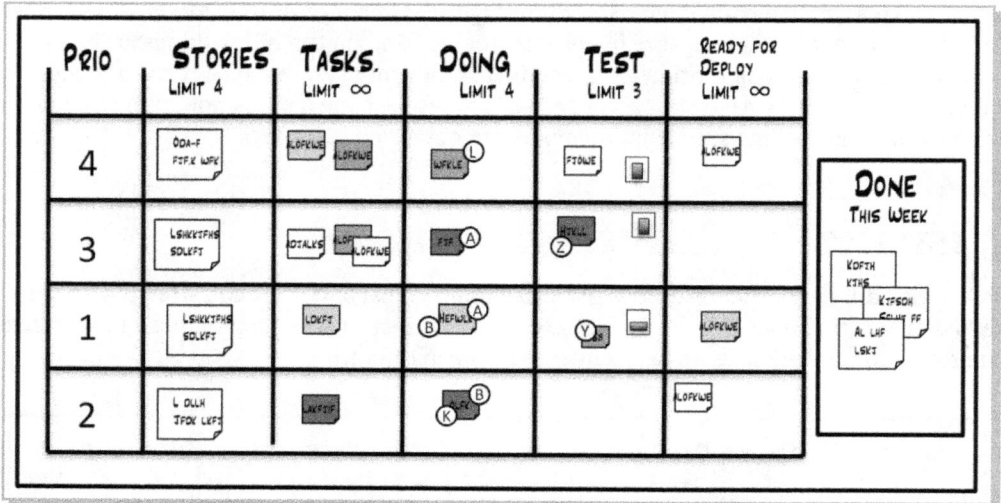

A Kanban board with stories broken down tasks

If you are not familiar with the word "story" in the context of Agile we will explain it for you briefly. The correct name is "user story" and is often used within Agile for a feature and is usually written in a format where you in one sentence get an understanding of:

➤ Who will benefit from this feature

➤ What the feature is

➤ Why it's valuable for that person or role

"Tasks" are the actual technical work that needs to be done to fulfill the value in the story. The numbers in the column "Prio" represent the stories prioritization. It could also be visualized by the order where the first row has priority number one and the second has priority number two and so on, but then we need to move the notes around whenever something is done. Also note that now columns are used both for showing status and for showing prioritization.

This example also introduces the limit of infinite. Our advice is not to use it too often but sometimes it just makes no sense to have limitations.

Examples of Kanban boards

A Kanban board can, and should, look different in order to visualize the work for the specificities of the situation you find yourself in. Be prepared to change the look of the board frequently in the beginning to find a style that suits you and is capable of adapting to your needs whenever the circumstances change. A good Kanban board helps you to know what work needs to be done and in what order. It also helps you see the weaknesses in your system. If the board can help you find where you have bottlenecks, you can focus your efforts on these areas and improve them.

To give you some inspiration as to what an effective Kanban board might look like, we will now give you some examples of boards that we have come across.

Kanban board example – internal operation

This example comes from an operation department hosting their own application. An ordinary day for them was a mix of daily duties, firefighting, and small projects to proactively reduce the numbers of fires. The daily duties were typically checking logs and remove old log files.

PRIO	TO DO	WORKING ON	DONE
URGENT	PROD, SMX, KJHF	QI	WOI
DAILY DUTY	SO, QOB, WER, SFS		
2	BUILD, ABA, TES HO	JKH	
3	SAOF SOJ, TES HO		
1	PERF, SO OB	SMX, DH	SFS, JFH, WER

A Kanban board for an internal operation department with three classes of services ("to do", "working on", and "done")

As you can see on the board this department has divided their work into three classes of services; urgent, daily duties, and proactive work. Urgent has the highest priority followed by daily duties. The proactive work was done when there were no urgent work to do and the daily duties were done. There could be three proactive projects ongoing in parallel and they had an internal strict prioritization, which was shown with a figure in the first column. Both urgent and proactive work was broken down into tasks.

Before introducing Kanban, this team spent most of their time fighting fires and doing the daily duties. They knew what was causing most of their fires but there were no time left for fixing the root cause of the problem since they had to spend all their time on minimizing the damage the problems caused. There were actually some time between the fires but that was spent on irrelevant things. Since they know there would soon be a new fire, they didn't want to start anything big that they would need to interrupt.

By setting up the board they achieved three very important things. The team was able to win the support and confidence of management. The Kanban board allowed, for example, management to see how many fires there were, which encouraged them to take the decision to make the investment in replacing hardware and software. The visual dimension of the Kanban board also ensured a certain degree of transparency and clarity about how the work was being done, which brought the confidence of the department manager. The board was a demonstration that the team was working effectively and that the necessary daily duties were taken care of.

It also ensured that the number of ongoing proactive work was limited and strictly prioritized so they got a good focus. When it was possible, between reactive work, everyone was working on the same proactive project at the same time.

Finally, because ongoing proactive work was effectively limited and strictly prioritized, the team had a strong focus on a specific task at any given time.

The result was fantastic. Those few moments of focused time spent on the most important proactive work were enough to remove one big source of fires. This gave them less urgent issues and more time on proactive work, which reduced the fires and gave them even more time to spend on proactive work. It became a positive loop. They got more control of the situation and they could produce value instead of reacting to problems, which led to a much better work situation.

Kanban board example – development team

The next example comes from a development team who are disciplined when it comes to breaking things down into small pieces of work.

ToDo	Developing Limit 4	Ready for Test. Limit 4	Test Limit 2	Done This Week

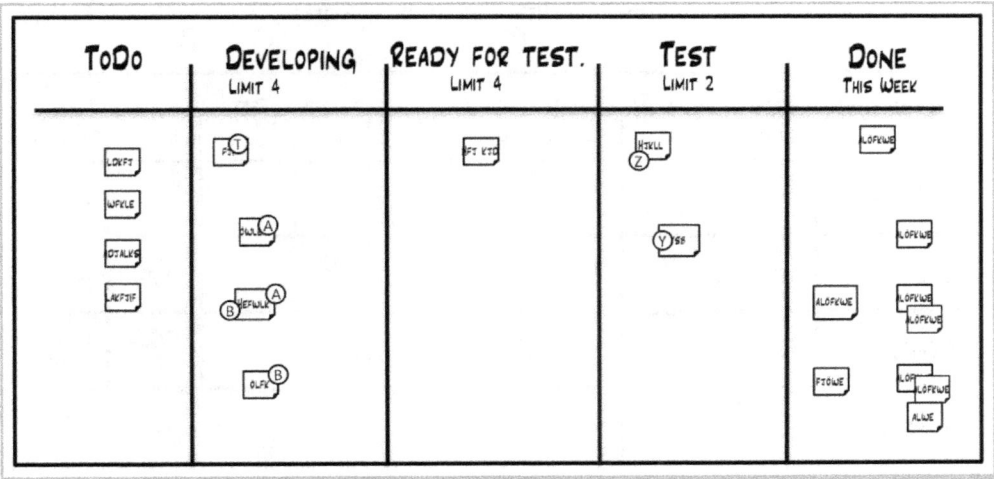

A very simple board with status columns and avatar magnets

A board does not need to be complicated—in fact, the simpler the better, as long as it helps the team.

If there is a need to handle very urgent issues there could be a good idea to have a special lane for them. The usual name for that class of service is **Expedite**. Another way of showing urgency is to have a special picture on top of them. A team that worked for the police authority had a police car to highlight work that was urgent.

It is very common is to use a pink or red note to show when something is stuck or waiting for something. If your board looks like a Christmas tree, full of red notes, you know you have problems. This is probably because:

➤ You are dependent on knowledge you do not have close

➤ You are dependent on other teams' work

➤ The workload is not well spread among the team members

➤ You are short of some resource you need, such as a test environment

➤ You start work without analyzing what is needed to fulfill the work

Different processes for different issue types

The board does not need to be a perfect matrix with all rows having all columns. Here comes an example of a board with different rows for different type of work. As you can see, defects and support have another process. This doesn't matter, as they can still be on the same board as the others. The purpose of the board is to make it easy to see the status, what you should do next, and where the problems in the flow are. If updating the board feels like an obligation and something that is draining the energy from the people involved, it has to be changed.

This figure shows a board that involves different kinds of work:

Type of work	Next Limit 6	Req.An. Limit 1	Ready For Dev. Limit 2	Dev Limit 3	Ready For Test Limit 2	Test Limit 2	Ready For Deploy Limit 2	Deploying Limit 3	Done This Week
Front End	KPD.M	PE (I)							LOPKWE
Back End	DKL		KLAOS	DWL (A)		REVLL Z		(K)(C)	LOPKWE
Defect	LDKFE WFKLE			(A) (B) FWLK		Y H		(L) ALOFKWE K	ALOFKWE LOFKWE
Support	OTALKE LAKFSF				(B) DUFE		OKTS KLWE	DLKS ALOFKWE	ALOFKWE

A board with different types of work

A board without rows and columns

The next example is interesting; it highlights the fact that, ultimately, a board can look like whatever you want it to look like. Don't feel limited by the examples here and the boards you see for other teams, fix a board that suites your team. The example here comes from a team that is working with signal enrichment in radio base stations. The idea came from a workshop where the team, together with an expert, went through the architecture for the upcoming development work. When the architecture was drawn on the whiteboard the team put up notes on the architectural drawing with what work was needed to complete the task. When this was done, one of the team members said: "Why not use the architectural schema as a board?" This is a great idea but we needed a way of showing the status. Another team member suggested showing the status by colored lines. A green line meant that the work was started and a red line meant that the work was done.

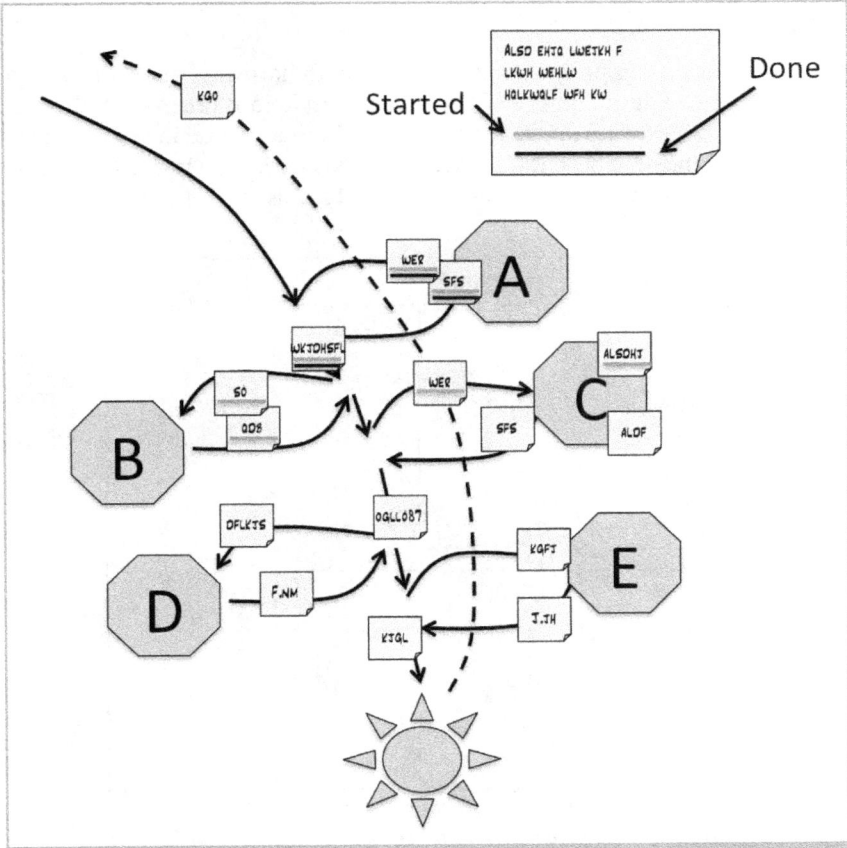

The architectural drawing has become a Kanban board where work is placed on it and the status is visualized with coloured lines on the notes

This way of showing what work there was to be done and the current status was very simple to get an overview of the system and the development status. As one developer put it, "This is the first time I fully understand and am truly interested in what everyone else is doing. I can see the function come true step by step on our white board."

A board for aggregated status

The next figure shows a company that is delivering both hardware and software and where the features need development of both. When an item is taken from the **Next** column it's split into hardware and software tasks. Those are done in separate teams and are integrated when they are both done. Each team has their own board to keep track of their work but here is the board to see the aggregated status for both teams:

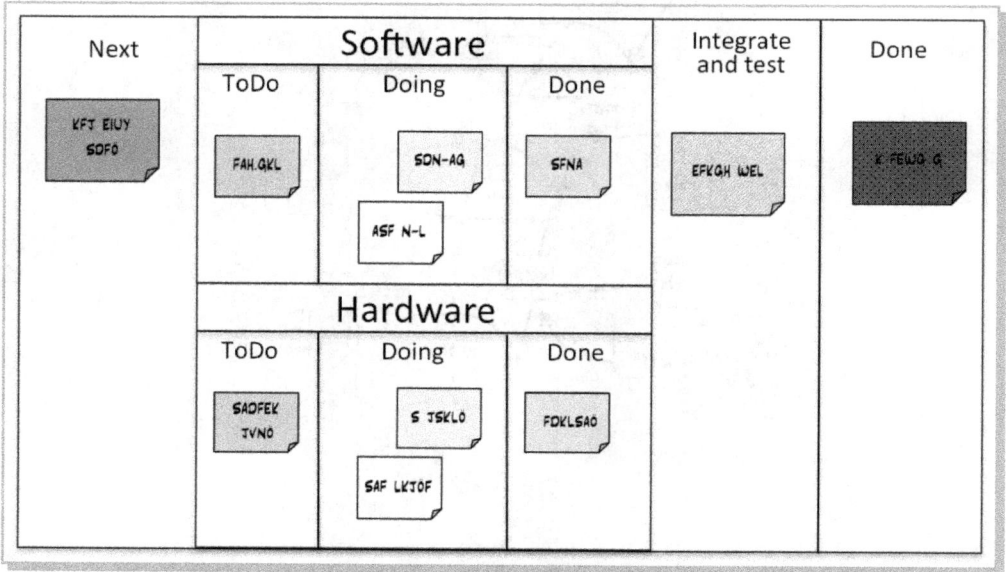

Next	Software			Integrate and test	Done
	ToDo	Doing	Done		
KFT EIUY SOFO	FAH.GKL	SON-AG / ASF N-L	SFNA	EFKGH WEL	K FEWG G
	Hardware				
	ToDo	Doing	Done		
	SAOFEK JVNO	S JSKLO / SAF LKTOF	FDKLSAO		

A blended Kanban board showing the aggregated status for multiple teams

Electronic versus physical boards

Should I use an electronic or physical Kanban board? Many teams choose to have either an electronic or a physical board. So which one should you choose? Here are the benefits of having an electronic board:

➤ No matter where you are you can always see the status and follow the progress

➤ This type of board works well for distributed teams

➤ It's possible to get reports

➤ It's possible to link to or contain more information on a note

There are several products for an electronic Kanban board. Here are a few of them:

➤ Pivotal tracker

➤ Jira Agile (former known as Jira+GreenHopper)

➤ Agile Zen

➤ Lean Kit

➤ Trello
➤ Target process
➤ Rally
➤ Web whiteboard

The last one, Web whiteboard, is the odd one in the list since it's just a painting area, just like a physical whiteboard and just like the physical version it has a lot of freedom and is easy to change.

Here are some benefits of using a physical whiteboard:

➤ The size improves visibility and helps you "see" the bottlenecks
➤ Easy to customize however you want
➤ Multiple people can edit the board simultaneously

So which one is the best? The tool is just a tool. Sometimes they are right in the context and sometimes they are wrong. The tool is not the problem; it's how it's used that is the problem. A hammer is great for nailing nails and a screwdriver is great for screws. You can use a hammer for a screw and a screwdriver for a nail but it's not a great tool for it. Let's look at some criteria for a good tool.

A good tool increases interaction

The first value of the Agile Manifesto is "individuals and interaction over processes and tools". A tool should help to improve communication and interaction between people with different skills and interests. It does it by visualizing what we need to communicate about. When it's obvious that we need to communicate to succeed we will communicate.

A good tool is flexible

The tool should be changed to support the team. The team should never need to change their way of working just to fit the tool.

We're not saying that it's impossible to get high energy in a team using only an electronic board but it seems to be much harder. We think the reason is that the electronic board:

➤ Is usually displayed on a screen that is smaller than a whiteboard
➤ Entering information in the tool becomes a bottleneck in meetings since only one person can control the input devices
➤ Does not invite people to walk around since it can be accessed from people's desk
➤ Limits important changes in the team's way of working since it's standardized
➤ People tend to get more interested in what they can do with the tool instead of what the team needs
➤ Managers draw conclusions from their desks without consulting the team

It seems to be something positive that happens with the team spirit when a bunch of people are gathered around a big board discussing a problem.

Summary

In this chapter we went through how to create a Kanban board. We started by collecting relevant information and visualization dimensions. We then matched them to use the best visualizers for the most important information. We went back to the value stream map we drew in the *Chapter 2 Days 3-5 – Getting to Know Your System*, and made the process on the board inlined with the process we had in the value stream map. We discovered that some steps could be skipped since no time was spent there.

We also showed Kanban boards that could handle different types of situations depending on whether the team works with operation, development, or is just keeping track on the projects at an aggregated level.

Finally we compared electronic and physical boards and found that physical boards have a lot of advantages, but that some situations give reason to use an electronic board as well.

In the next chapter you will learn why limits are important for quick delivery. You will also learn an exercise you can do with your teams to help them understand the importance as well.

>4

Days 10-11 – Setting the Limits

You should, by now, have a pretty good understanding of your process and a Kanban board that supports it. We will now spend two days on deciding the limits to start with. Setting effective limits is integral to Kanban; it is often ignored, but to do so threatens the results that you are hoping Kanban will allow you to achieve.

Kanban is about limiting the work to make sure task switching is kept to a minimum and to stop buffers from being built up inside your system. Buffers make work grow old and become outdated. Value is lost in those internal queues while the frustration from the stakeholders increases.

The best way to acknowledge the importance of setting limits is through a simple game. All you need are matches or sticks, dice, and five people to play. You can do this with three to six people, but in this example, we will use five. If you have more than six people, you can have multiple setups of three to six people. You are then able to aggregate their results and get an average that gets closer to a theoretical outcome. Because of the uncertainty of dice, there is a small risk that a single setup gives an unexpected result.

Together, you form a system with five stations. Each station has a capacity of 1 to 6 depending on the value of their dice. In front of the first player there is an unlimited queue of sticks. The roles in the following diagram are just examples to better illustrate the system:

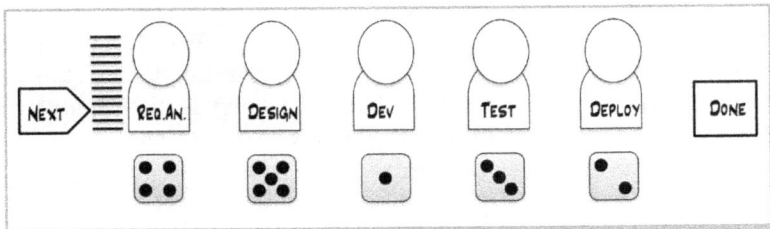

The setup at the beginning

At first, everyone rolls the dice so we get the first set of numbers for the players. The first move is for everyone to move as many sticks they can, depending on the eyes of the dice and how many sticks there are in front (that is, upstream) of you. Mathematically, that could be written as min (eyes of the dice, buffer upstream before moving). We have included the mathematical formula for those of you who would like to write a program to simulate the game:

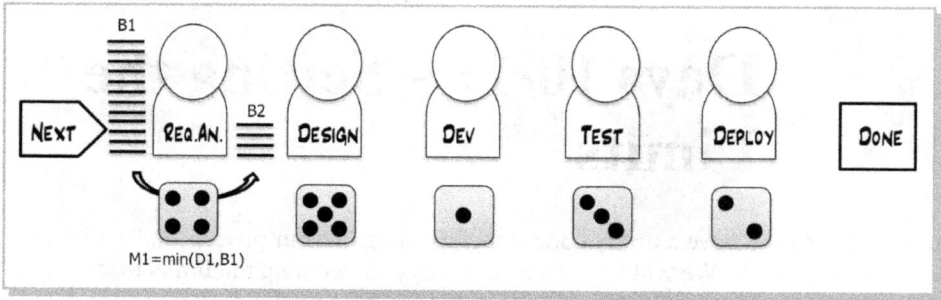

This is how it looks after the first round (M=Move, D=Dice, B=Buffer)

The designer can't move anything in this first round since the buffer upstream was empty when the round started.

The next step is for all the players to roll the dice again and move accordingly:

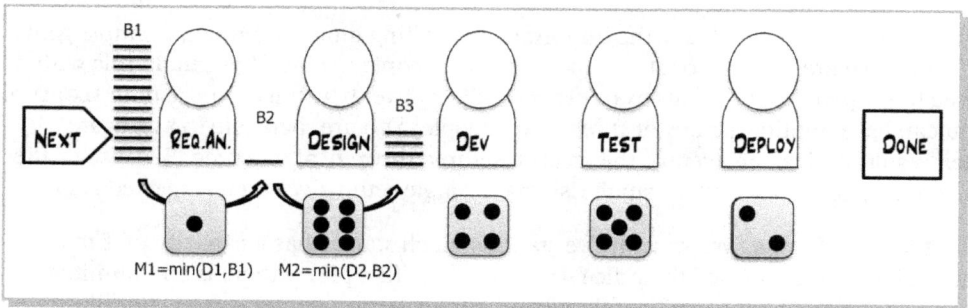

How it looks after two rounds

In the example, you can see that the move for the second player (**M2**) is four and not six as the dice (**D2**) is showing. This is because the upstream buffer (**B2**) only contains four sticks when the round starts. Move simultaneously to make sure that no stick passes two persons in the same round. An alternative is that the last person, the deploy person in this example, moves first and the other follows one by one.

Keep doing this for 20 rounds.

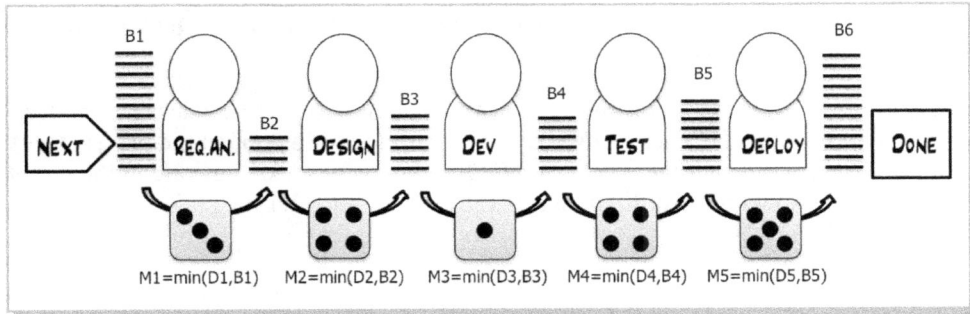

How it looks after 20 rounds

After 20 rounds, you should count how much work you have been able to complete, that is, how many sticks you have after the last person (in **B6**). This is your throughput or capacity, how much you can produce in 20 rounds. Write this down for later use.

The next step is to find your time to market. The 20 first rounds set the table and filled your buffers. To find out your time to market, you need to see how many rounds are needed to clear the table. Roll the dice once more, and bring sticks in according to the dice just like before. This will be the last time the first person brings sticks in and all the sticks from **B1** are put back into their box.

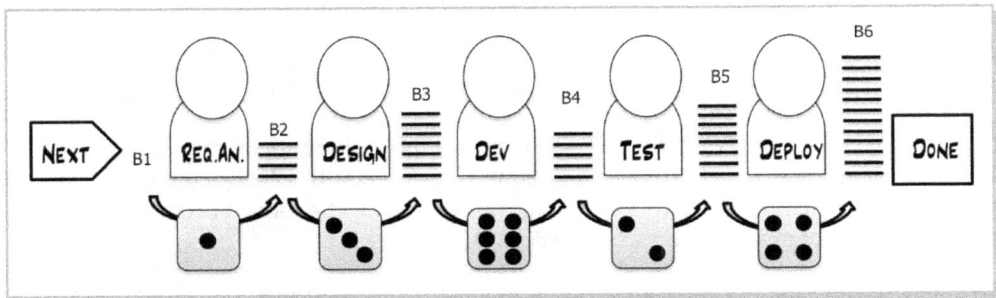

How it looks after 1 round in the second step

The players keep rolling dice until all the sticks have passed the last person. The number of rounds needed to do so is your time to market. You already wrote down your capacity after 20 rounds, now you should write down how many rounds were needed to clear the table including the round that was the last when you brought new sticks in. Since this is how many rounds it took for the last stick you brought in to pass the whole system, it is your time to market.

These figures are of no interest unless you can compare them with something. To get something to compare with, you need to do exactly the same, but this time you will be using limits of six.

Adding limits

The limits are that a player is only allowed to move sticks that make the buffer to the next player less or equal to the limit.

Since the limit is six sticks, it means that you can only have one to six sticks in a buffer (between two people) after everybody has done their move. How much the player (**Dev**) can move depends on what the dice shows (**D3**), how many sticks there are in the buffer before (**B3**), and how much room there is in the buffer after, after the player downstream has moved (**X4**).

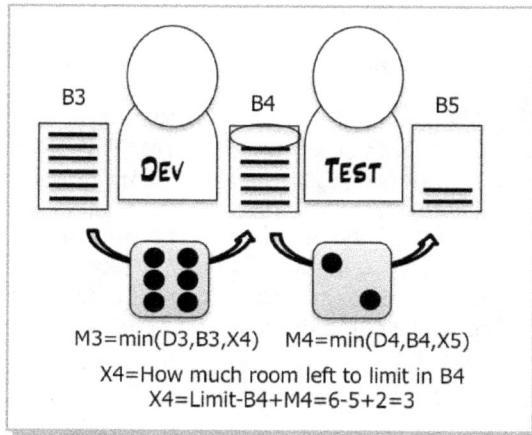

M3=min(D3,B3,X4)   M4=min(D4,B4,X5)
X4=How much room left to limit in B4
X4=Limit-B4+M4=6-5+2=3

The mathematical explanation of how much the Dev person can move. Before this round, B4 contained 5 sticks (1 left to the limit of 6). Two of them are moved by the tester, which gives 3 for the developer to move.

In the preceding example, the Dev person can only move three sticks, even when the dice is showing six eyes. One stick because the size of the buffer, before the move, was only five while the limit is six (6-5=1). Two more sticks can be moved because the player downstream will move two according to dice **D4**.

This may sound rather complicated, but in practice, the easiest method is that the last person moves first. The second last person will then easily see how much he/she can move and so on until the first person has moved and it's time for the next round.

Showing the result in a graph

When you have done the second step, you should have a new figure for capacity and time to market. The following diagram shows the result plotted in a graph:

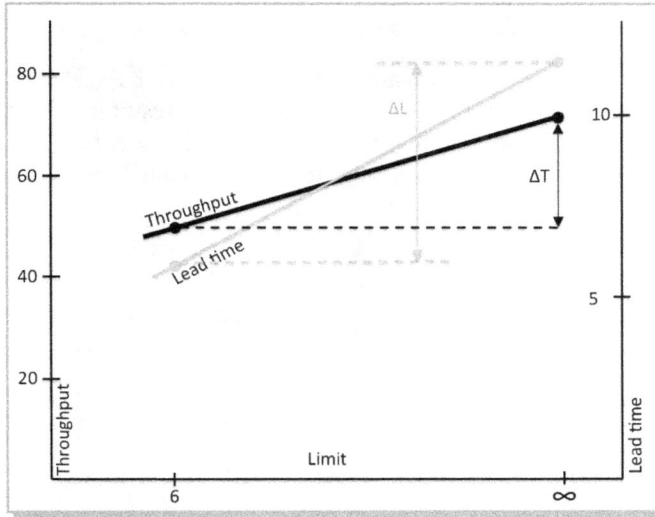

The game's result put in a graph. As you can see, the lead time shrinks more than the throughput when introducing limits.

Theoretically, there should be a big difference in time to market (ΔL) and a small difference in throughput (ΔT). Practically, this is not always the result due to the big variation in personal capacity, 1-6. If you have four teams or more doing this exercise, your average result will most likely get close to the theoretical outcome.

The time to run this exercise is about 30 minutes.

You can make a tweak to the exercise to get a more obvious result. What you can do is generate a bottleneck by reducing the capacity for the second user. Divide the second user's dice result by 2, rounded up, so if the dice shows 4, he or she moves only 2 sticks, and if the dice shows 5, then he or she moves 3 sticks. If you happen to have dice showing 1-3, that is just as good. After 20 rounds, you should now have a big buffer in front of the second player, and it will take many rounds before the board is empty.

Run the game once more but with a limit of 4 on the buffers between players. Present the result on the board, preferably in a spreadsheet projected on the wall. Here is an example of how it can look when three teams have run the exercise:

	Team 1		Team 2		Team 3		AVG	
	TP	TTM	TP	TTM	TP	TTM	AVG TP	AVG TTM
1) No bottleneck, no limit	51	10	55	5	49	6	51,67	7,00
2) No bottleneck, limit	48	4	49	5	49	3	48,67	4,00
	-6%	-60%	-11%	0%	0%	-50%	-6%	-43%
3) Bottleneck, no limit	32	20	32	21	27	24	30,33	21,67
4) Bottleneck, limit	29	7	27	7	29	4	28,33	6,00
	-9%	-65%	-16%	-67%	7%	-83%	-7%	-72%

The result is hopefully astonishing. If it's not, you have probably just been unlucky with the dice, so run it again.

Simulating the result

If you know how to program or if you are an advanced user of Excel (or any other spreadsheet program for that matter), you can simulate the result instead of testing it. In the following graph, you can see the result of a simulation where 5 players are running 100 rounds and where the limit was changed between 3 and 100:

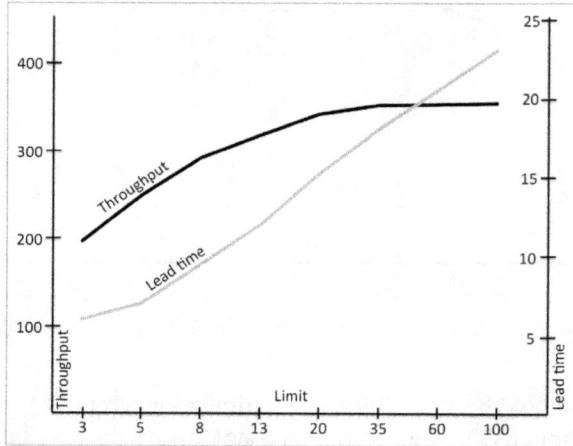

The graph shows the result of a data simulation

The interesting result is shown in the following table:

Changing limit	Difference in throughput	Difference in time to market
100 to 5	-31%	-70%
100 to 8	-19%	-59%
100 to 13	-12%	-48%
100 to 20	-5%	-34%

This means that if you set the limit to 20, you lose only 5 percent on throughput, but you will be done in much less time. If time to market is really important for you, you can set the limit to 5 and be done much quicker.

What limit should you start with?

It's now time to decide which limit to begin with. Without running for a time, it's very hard to predict what would be the best balance between throughput and lead-time. Your first decision is about how important quick time to market is for you. If it is very important, we suggest you start with tough (low) limits. In practice, that means that the normal is that people are waiting for work instead of work waiting for people to take care of it. In other words, you want the next work station/process step to be ready to start working when you are ready with your part of the work.

If time to market is not very important, you can start with wider limits and allow some buffers to build up between process steps just to make sure everybody almost always has something to do.

The reasons for having queues between process steps is to have a buffer to handle variation caused either by different work capacity, like in the match game previously, or different amounts of work.

A good flow is created by slack, that is, the time when some people actually have nothing to do. This time could be used to improve their own way of working or helping others who at the moment have more to do.

Limits do not need to be digital, either it's one or it's zero, in the way that as long as you are under the limit, it's fine to add more work until we reach the limit and then absolutely nothing more. Instead, we suggest you have the last available queue places saved for extreme cases. This gives pressure to have the smallest possible limits but be able to handle cases of extreme variation. In the following example, there is a hard limit of 4 but a soft limit of 3:

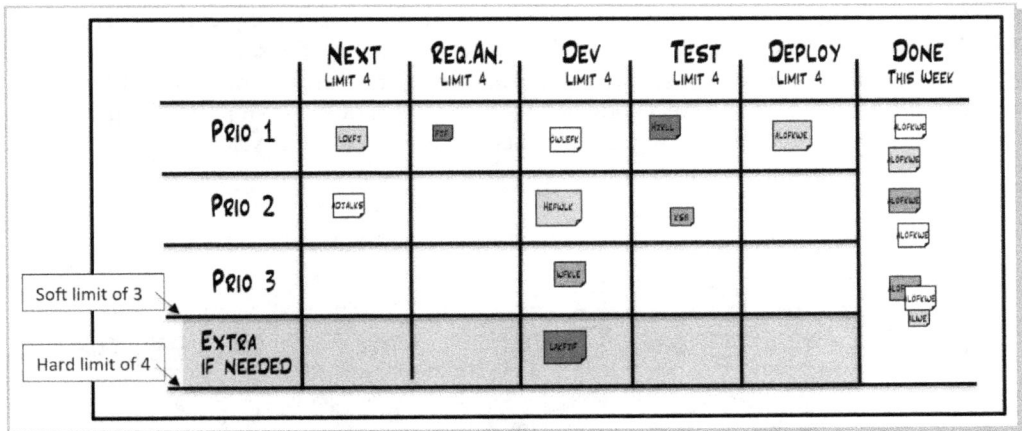

	NEXT LIMIT 4	REQ.AN. LIMIT 4	DEV LIMIT 4	TEST LIMIT 4	DEPLOY LIMIT 4	DONE THIS WEEK
PRIO 1	[card]	[card]	[card]	[card]	[card]	[card] [card]
PRIO 2	[card]		[card]	[card]		[card] [card]
PRIO 3			[card]			[cards]
EXTRA IF NEEDED			[card]			

Soft limit of 3
Hard limit of 4

A Kanban board with a hard limit of 4 and a soft limit of 3

Minimum limits

We have also seen teams using a minimum limit, that is, a signal to tell that there is not enough work for the station. This is used to level out the flow. The minimum limit becomes a signal that we should help the workstation up.06

m not because they are reaching the maximum limit, but because there is a risk of the ketchup effect, first comes nothing and then everything comes.

For teams that have been working some time with limits, the limit itself is not of the most important thing; it is instead much more important to see the whole picture and start discussions about how to level out the workflow and improve the flow.

Theory of constraints

Theory of constraints is a management philosophy introduced and described in the book *The Goal*, Eliyahu M. Goldratt, 1984. Part of the theory is a step-by-step guide to find and eliminate bottlenecks to get an improved total flow.

Using elements from the theory of constraints in combination with the notion of limits taken from Kanban, we will show you how to optimize flow throughout an organization.

Step 1 – identify the bottleneck

Identify the system's constraint or bottleneck. Bottlenecks are easy to find; they are directly after a queue of work. If you don't believe that, just think about it the next time you are in a queue yourself. It could be in traffic or in line waiting to enter an event. After a long time in the queue, you pass the bottleneck and the queue is gone and the speed increases. You actually enter a part of the system where there is slack, that is, over capacity, or in the case of a road, some room between you and the other cars.

To visualize what we're talking about, we borrow the setup from the previous example, but with one difference; the dice are fixed so the capacity stays the same all the time. In the following example, you see what happens when one step becomes the bottleneck (**Dev** in the example) when everybody just works with his or her own parts. We get long queues of requirements and design documents just waiting to be developed.

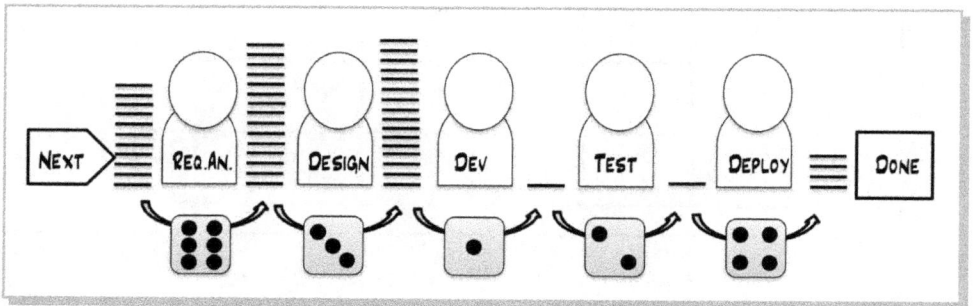

A system where "Dev" is the bottleneck and everybody works with full capacity as long as there is something to do. As you can see, there is a buffer within the system before both "Dev" and "Design".

Step 2 – align all other steps according to the bottleneck

Set limits to the process steps before the bottleneck so that no or minimal queues are built up before the bottleneck. In the road example, that could mean to force cars into one line before the bottleneck. We know this sounds counterproductive, but you will soon understand why. For software development, the solution could be to reduce the limits even harder to give the bottleneck some overcapacity to be spent on improving themselves. Now look at the pictures, the previous one (without limits) and the following one (with limits).

They have the same output since that is according to the capacity of the bottleneck. The difference is the time to market. The time that passes from when the requirement analysis starts to work on something until it's deployed is a lot shorter.

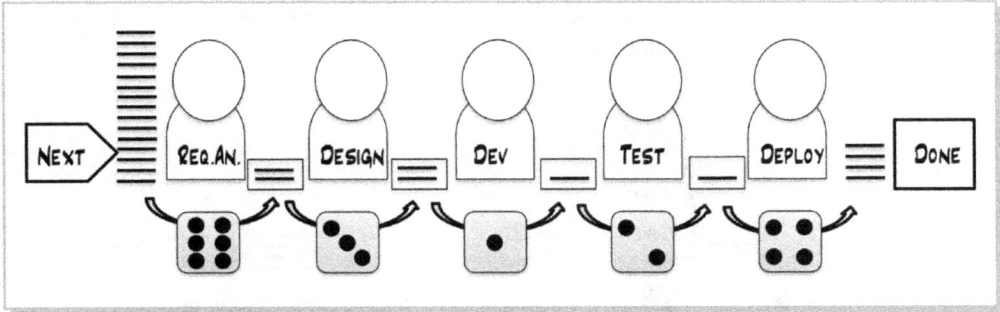

The same situation as in step 1 but with limits to hinder queues from building up. Without changing throughput, the buffers within the system before both "Dev" and "Design" are gone.

You may argue that we have only moved the work to the place before the requirement analysis—and you'd be correct. The thing is that in the quickly changing world we live in, some or even most of the work waiting untouched outside our system has already reached its best before date and needs either to be updated (analyzed again) or thrown away. The likelihood that we will re-evaluate work that has already entered the system decreases the more we work on it. We risk spending expensive development time on something that will not bring enough value back.

Step 3 – increase the capacity through the bottleneck

The next step is to improve the flow through the bottleneck. Often there is a grey zone about who does what between the process steps. The process steps before and after the bottleneck could do more of the work in the grey zone. It's important that the initiative to improve the flow through the bottleneck is an organizational effort for everyone, no matter role or title, to care about and to solve.

Visualizing the total flow and its bottlenecks is motivating people to change their behavior. When everybody understands that a wider bottleneck is good for the total flow, for the company and for everyone, the motivation for helping the bottleneck will hopefully be higher. That's why it's so important to visualize the flow so everyone can see the bottleneck with his or her own eyes. In the next picture, we continue the example but move some capacity to the bottleneck:

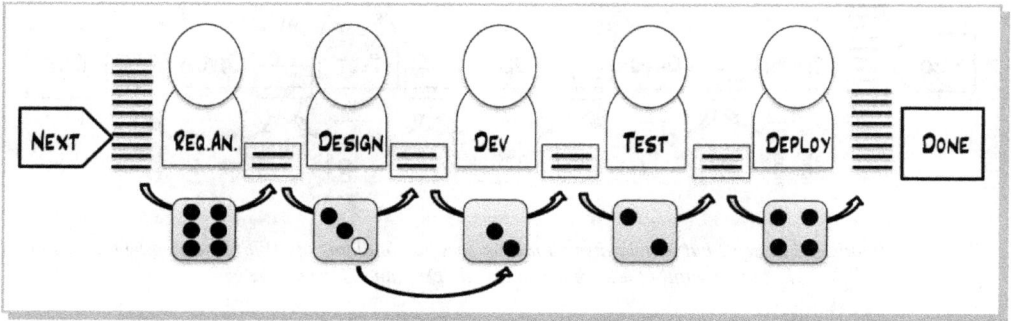

The same situation as in step 2 but where "Design" helps "Dev" to become more productive.

Here comes an example of what you can do if the test step is the bottleneck. Usually, a lot of time is spent on setting up a test environment with relevant test data and getting an understanding about which areas need to be changed and need retesting. This is typically a grey zone. Both developers and testers can do this, but if testing is the bottleneck, it's wise that developers set up the environment with data according to the need the testers express. Then testers and developers sit together to walk through the changes. The handover from developers to testers is done in a dialog instead of just written documents.

Another example to improve test capacity is to automate a lot of tests so developers can be more comfortable that delivered functionality has no defects. Testers will then spend less time reporting defects and retest them later on when they are fixed.

Step 4 – start over from step 1

Start over again to find your new bottleneck. Every system has a bottleneck. When you fix one, there is always a new one to be found and fixed. The forth step is to start over again at step 1 to find the next bottleneck.

Summary

In this chapter, you learned how to play a game to help your organization understand the importance of using limits. We saw that limits made a small decrease of overall capacity but a big improvement on the time to market or lead-time, which it's also called.

You also learned how to find and remove bottlenecks by using four steps. This is a method inspired by the theory of constraint management philosophy.

In the next chapter, you will learn which roles you need and which meetings you should have.

>5

Day 12 – Choosing the Roles and Meetings You Need

You are now close to your first day of Kanban. The only thing left to do is choose the right roles and meetings to adopt, in order to achieve a smooth application of Kanban. This could be a very short chapter, as Kanban does not prescribe any roles or meetings. It's even explicitly written in Kanban's foundational principles that you should initially not change the way of working or the roles.

Kanban's foundational principles are:

> ➤ Start with what you do now

> ➤ Agree to pursue evolutionary change

> ➤ Initially, respect current roles, responsibilities, and job titles

> ➤ Encourage acts of leadership at all levels

The reason for not changing is to minimize the risk of getting drawbacks in the middle of the change process.

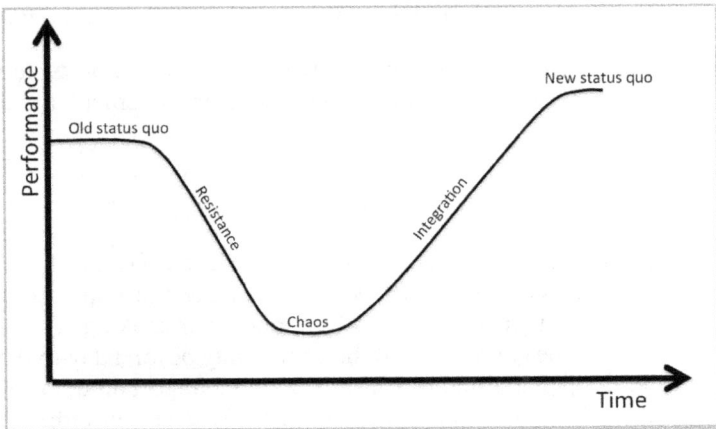

Change in performance during a change process

According to Virginia Satir's change process model, every change in the organization may even be expected to result in a drop in performance. The biggest risk is that some high manager sees this performance drop while the organization is in the chaos phase and demands a change back to the old status quo. The problem is that is also a change, which will most likely result in an even worse performance drop.

To avoid major drops in performance, Kanban's fundamental principles tell you to take it easy with unmotivated initial changes. Instead, by visualizing and measuring, the changes that we decide to do will be motivated and the resistance from the organization less damaging.

Introducing new roles

If and when you decide that you want to make some changes, perhaps to improve the workflow, some roles that you could look into are explored in the following section, and maybe add or change them. To get a lean organization, only add the roles that you really need and modify them to suit your organization and modify them again when the situation changes.

Kanban Master

Kanban Master is a role that is borrowed from Scrum where the Scrum Master is prescribed in the Scrum Guide. Since there is no defined role called Kanban master you can define it yourself, but if you want to follow the recommendations from Scrum, the following sections explore what a Kanban master will do.

Master of the process

The Kanban Master should make sure the team follows the few rules of Kanban and makes the most out of them. Kanban is not telling you what your process should look like but instead telling you to have an explicit process and why that will help you. The Kanban Master should make sure that the team knows their process and also follow it.

A good Kanban Master helps the team visualize their process and how to spot the bottlenecks. They know that Kanban is about continuous improvement and do their best to convey this.

Servant leader

The Kanban Master is also a **servant leader** to the team. The term comes from Robert K. Greenleaf and can be described like this: a servant leader treats the employees with great respect in order to make them grow and be involved in decision-making. They also do work for the good of the people, the company, and the community beyond day-to-day realities. A servant leader believes openness and persuasion are more important than control. They facilitate meetings and help the others to contribute and take decisions rather than doing that themselves.

Shielding the team

Most people prefer to work focused on one thing without being interrupted by questions from the organization. At the same time we need to have good interaction with the organization to understand the business, be involved early, develop the right products, get quick response to our questions and maybe most importantly, contribute with our knowledge before decisions are made on wrong assumptions.

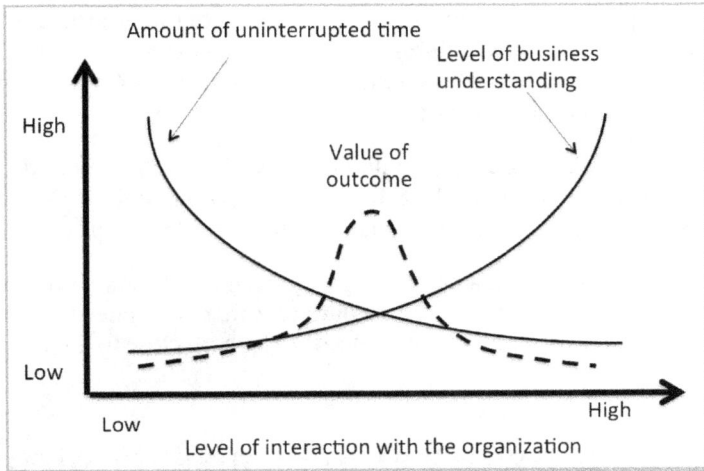

The balance between too much and too little interaction with the organization

As you can see, there is a sweet spot somewhere between too much and too little interaction. It's typically for the Kanban Master to help with this hard balancing act. The first thing should be to find the difference between good and bad interaction and that the difference depends on timing, content, how it's performed, and many other things. Let me give an example: if someone starts a discussion at an already schedule meeting, the interruption is minimal, but if the same message is screamed out at the office, the interruption is much worse.

Product owner

Another role that is common to see in organizations doing Kanban is the product owner or **product champion**. Since Kanban is not prescribing any roles, you should only have a product owner if you already have one, and you believe it's good for your workflow, or you have concluded from your continuous improvement that your system will benefit from having one.

To give you some hints about what a product owner can do, once again we lend the description from Scrum.

The prime responsibility for the product owner is to manage the incoming flow to make sure the people working in the system know what to do and in which order. The input of work tasks is probably coming from many different sources, which needs to be prioritized. Each of these sources has stakeholders who probably care the most about the work they want the team to do. A good product owner manages to prioritize in a way that the result gives the highest possible value in each moment and that the stakeholders are most satisfied with the work done by the team.

To achieve this, the product owner must be transparent with the prioritizations and should keep the backlog, the Next column at the board, visual for everyone interested. The stakeholder who is not satisfied with the prioritizations is then able to approach the product owner to discuss another order.

The product owner has also a great possibility to grow motivation within the team by communicating the vision of the product. If this vision is compelling, the members of the team will be more motivated to reach the goals that are clear steps towards the vision.

The product owner can also act as a customer proxy. That is a person who is sitting close to the people doing the work, and can answer questions that are related to customer value. To be able to achieve this, the product owner needs to be both close to the team and close to the customers.

Chief product owner and/or project manager

For big companies where there are many teams working in parallel, there is a need to synchronize and prioritize between systems or teams to reduce the risk of sub optimization. This could either be handled by a round table group of product owners or by an appointed person. This person could be called the chief **product owner**.

Generally it's a good idea to let the same people handle all the development of a product irrespective of whether the organization prefers to call the work part of a project or part of maintenance. People working with a project that has a clear end, have a tendency to build products that are less efficient to maintain and operate. This sub-optimization causes high costs later in the product life cycle and is something that absolutely needs to be eliminated. Having the same people working with all initiatives for developing and operating the product, will give them knowledge and understanding of the whole life cycle and hopefully that will help them reduce maintenance and operational costs.

A common setup for big companies where maintenance and projects are developed by the same people is to have a project manager that takes care of the project and a chief product owner who decides the periodization between projects, and between projects and maintenance.

Cross-functional or specialized team

While Scrum tells you to have cross-functional teams, in Kanban you only have it if you believe it will improve your workflow. In a cross-functional team you have all the knowledge that is needed to fulfill an item that is in a backlog, from an idea to working software. The opposite is to have teams that only handle one or a few steps in the process. Teams that only handle one step are commonly called **skill teams** since they contain people with one and the same skill.

There are advantages with both models. Within the skill teams, people can help each other within their profession. They tend to get deeper in their knowledge. Cross-functional teams, on the other hand, are better at communicating between skills and tend to get a better view of the big picture. Both models have a need for communication on both skill and process level. One level will be solved by how the people are physically sitting together and overhearing each other. Virtual teams or forums can handle the other level. If you are organized in skill teams you need to have a forum to discuss the process and if you are organized in cross-functional teams, responsible for the whole process, you need forums where the people can discuss best practices within their skill.

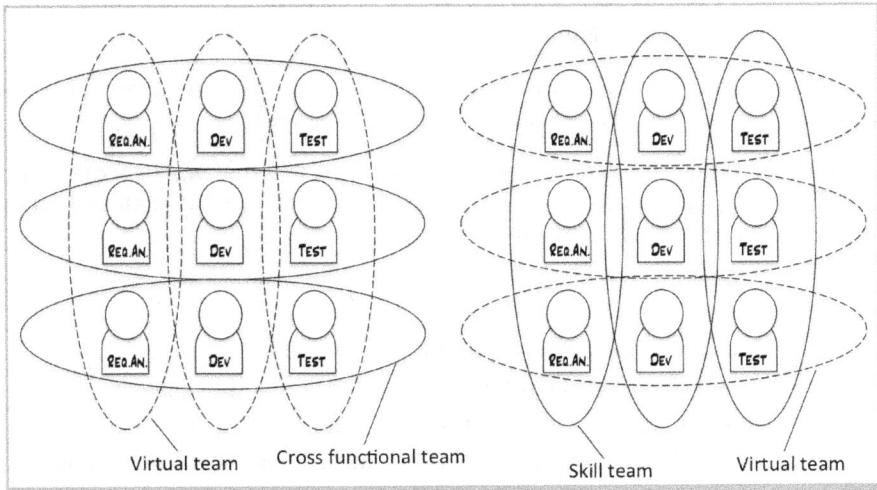

Cross-functional teams versus skill teams

What works better? It depends on the situation, but we have found that it's harder to get communication working between skills than within a skill. That's why it's usually better to organize along the process in cross-functional teams and use forums to handle communication within a skill.

Meetings in Kanban

Kanban is a way of driving change, and is not a process, so no meetings are prescribed. We will provide some ideas for meetings you could have anyway. See it as a smorgasbord from where you can pick what you like.

Planning a meeting

Choosing the right product(s) to do next is an important and hard issue. Picking things in the wrong order might increase the risk level or damage the project, the product, or in the worst case scenario the whole company. Even if you have a product owner (see earlier in this chapter) it could be hard for one person to make the decision. From Jeff Patton comes the idea to bring more skills in to make the decision. What he calls "discovery group" includes individuals with knowledge of:

➤ Customer value

➤ User experience

➤ A developer who knows whether it is easy or hard or even impossible to develop a particular feature of a product

When these three skills get together to make the decision about priority, you have a good chance to develop things in the right order.

Another way is to bring someone or everyone from each skill that will be working on the feature, to the planning meeting. This is a good way to get all aboard at an early stage, which is also the reason for the next meeting.

Make a note

Brief about planning a meeting:

- **When**: When plans are needed or need to be change
- **Length**: 15 minutes per day to plan
- **Who**: Enough knowledge to understand value, cost, and risk
- **Purpose**: To decide in which order you should do the work to get maximum value and minimum risk

Story start meeting

When it's time to bring some new work in, we have seen great improvement in efficiency for companies that use story start meetings. It's a meeting only focused on one feature or story. Everybody who will be involved in the work or who has important information about the work is invited to this meeting.

Make a note

Brief about story start meeting:

- **When**: When it's time to start with a new story, feature or initiative that is not well known
- **Length**: About 60 minutes
- **Who**: Everybody who will be involved in the work or who has important information about the work
- **Purpose**: To get a broad understanding of the work that is about to be done

Daily sync

This is a daily meeting to identify things that are stopping the flow. It's not like the Scrum daily meeting where everyone is talking about what they have accomplished and plan to accomplish during the day. The Kanban version focuses only on the problems and who can be a part of fixing them. The meeting should not take more than fifteen minutes so there is no time for discussions. They will instead continue after the meeting with only the people who have the problem and the ones who can fix them. To minimize the risk for longer discussions everybody participating in the meeting should stand up. The hope is that tired legs will make their owners complain if someone steals too much time.

Make a note

Brief about the daily sync:

- **When**: At the same time every day
- **Length**: 15 minutes
- **Who**: Everybody who will be involved in the work
- **Purpose**: To identify and form a working group to solve problems that are stopping the daily flow

Enterprise sync

Big companies do usually have many development units, which are dependent on each other. Lack of communication between units is one of the most common reasons for the failure of projects. The enterprise sync is a meeting to improve communication between units and handles things such as:

- ➤ Corporate or organizational impediments
- ➤ Status against integration points
- ➤ Changes that other units may need to know
- ➤ What we are doing or have learned that could be of interest for other units

The meeting should be short (so stand up) and only talk enough to identify interesting topics to talk more about after the meeting and only with people who are interested.

Make a note

Brief about the enterprise sync:

- **When**: 1-5 times a week
- **Length**: 15 minutes
- **Who**: At least one person from every development unit
- **Purpose**: To avoid causing unpleasant surprises for each other, to learn from each other, and take advantage of each others' work

Demo meeting

The demo is a meeting to show the stakeholders what has been developed. In big companies this is more of a show where the information is one-way directed from the team to the audience without interaction. Since each team's demo should be very short it's possible to squeeze in up to 8 development units during a one-hour demo, which makes it a very efficient way to inform a big audience of what is happening in the company.

Make a note

Brief about the demo:

- **When**: Every 2-4 week
- **Length**: 1 hour
- **Who**: Everybody interested in the development work that is going on
- **Purpose**: To show what has been developed since the last demo

Review meeting

The review is almost like the demo but is performed in front of a smaller audience and has as its purpose to get feedback about the product and the new features. For companies running demos as described previously, it's a great combination to have reviews like a fair, immediately after the demo, to show more details and have a dialog about how the new features are working. All feedback should be taken care of and be prioritized in such way that you always develop the highest value at any time.

Make a note

Brief about the review:

- **When**: Every 2-4 week or when you have access to customers, stakeholders or end users
- **Length**: The time it takes
- **Who**: Everybody deeply interested in the development work that is going on
- **Purpose**: To get feedback on the product and newly developed features

Retrospective meeting

The most important meeting in Kanban is the retrospective since this is where we have time to focus on discussing improvements. Retrospectives can be done in many different ways and our recommendation is to vary and not use one version too many times in a row. We will talk about three common variations and we encourage you to vary your retrospectives and try different variants.

Some good books to read to get ideas how you can vary your retrospectives are:

> *Game storming* by Dave Gray, Sunni Brown and James Macanufo
> *Agile Retrospectives: Making Good Teams Great* by Esther Derby and Diana Larsen

Make a note

Brief about the retrospective:

- **When**: Every 2-4 week or when needed
- **Length**: 1.5 hours
- **Who**: Everybody involved in the development unit
- **Purpose**: To find ways to improve the process or sometimes even the organization

The plus-minus-delta retrospective

In this type of retrospective the participants write notes about what they think has been good and what has been less good during a given timeframe, usually since the last retrospective. They also write down ideas of changes to make the process better.

One way of doing this is to ask the participants to write notes for all three categories and then, when everyone is done, present them. Another way, and the way we prefer, is to start with and only focus on the category of good things. As soon as someone has written a note they get up and walk to the board, put the note there, and tell everyone about what they think has been good.

This immediate show and tell inspires others to write notes. When all notes are presented and no one is writing new notes it is time to open the next category, the one with what has been less good. At the same time you open the third category, the one with suggested improvements. You know you are working with good people when a note in the not-so-good category generates a few notes in the improvement category and maybe also a note in the good column written by someone who thinks that the same thing actually was good. A lot of activity with constructive discussions is good for improvements.

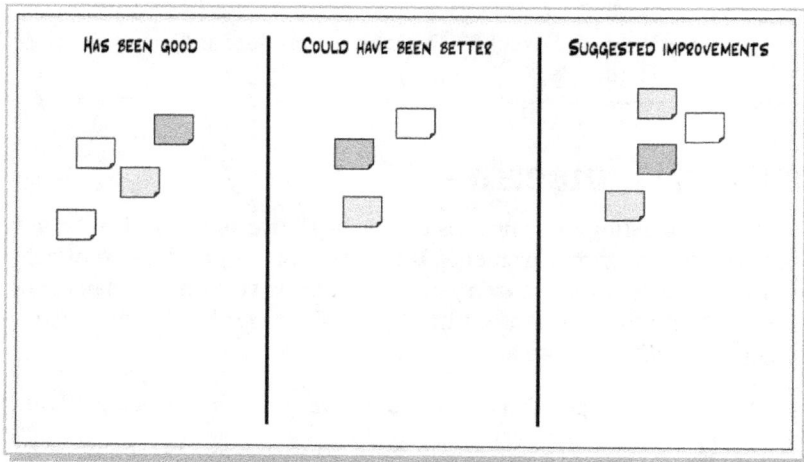

Typical board after a plus-minus-delta retrospective

Futurespective

The next variation of retrospective is good for development units where there is tension in the air or when there is a need for variation. It is like time travel and simulates the scenario where you have just completed a fantastic time frame. Everything has worked just the way it should have. The question is: what did we do to make it work so well?

You start this simulation by saying that today is March 15 even though it's actually February 15 and you have just had a fantastic month. Everything was just perfect. The reason why we are here is to learn from this success. The participants are then asked to write notes that complete the sentence: "I think it worked so well because ...", put them on the board, and present what they have written.

We like this variation because it stimulates another part of your brain than the plus-minus-delta variation. It has more innovation in it and it's fun to take time journeys. It's also less emotional because there is no blaming. It's just congratulating people for their new and better behavior.

The perfection game

The third variant of retrospective is the perfection game. The participants should grade the past time frame on a scale from 1 to 10 where 10 is perfect. They should then write notes about what made it worth the grade and what should have been done differently to make it worth a 10. This is preferably done in small clusters of 4-5 people in combination with a start of five minutes of their own to think for themselves. Some people need alone time and some people need discussion time. This helps both needs to be met. After the discussions the groups present their conclusions.

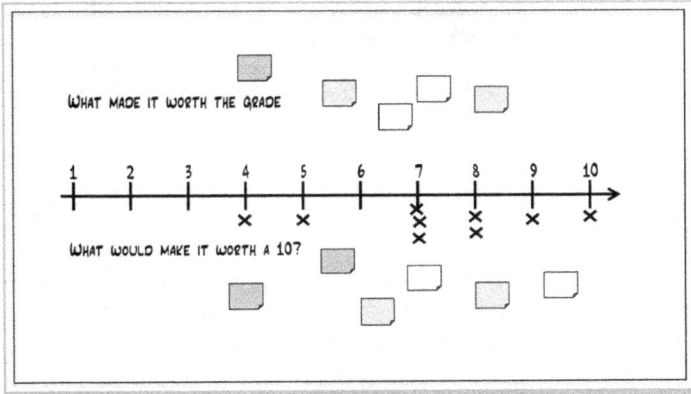

Typical board from a perfection game retrospective

Summarizing retrospectives

Even though there is a value in reflecting over the past there is even more value in getting a prioritized list of improvements that has a wide support within the group and the organization. To get this you need to include the part where you create this list at the end of your retrospective.

One way you can do this is by having the participants vote on the topics, either on things that need improvement or suggested improvements that they think should get the most attention. Collect those things in a prioritized list according to the votes. If there are no suggestions for improvements you need to spend time generating them, for instance with a brainstorming session.

Voting is not the same as consensus and in some situations it's very important to have everyone supporting the improvement. You can get a consensus by putting all topics above a line that you have drawn on the board, and ask the participants to move topics below the line if they don't agree that this is something that needs to be changed. Only the ones who moved the topic below the line are allowed to move it back again. At the end of the consensus session everyone supports all notes above the line. Now you can vote to decide the prioritizing of the notes.

By combining voting and consensus you get a prioritized list that is supported by everyone.

Warming up before a retrospective

Before a retrospective session it's good to warm up. A good warm up part refreshes your memory about what has happened during the time frame and it's a neutral start where everyone feels comfortable contributing. It's important to get everyone activated early. Studies have shown that if a participant has not said anything during the first five minutes they will not be very active during the rest of the session. We recommend you have a facilitator to help engage the quiet ones.

A warm-up session can be to draw a time line for the time frame you will talk about. The participants will then write notes about what happened during the time frame. It's neutral and without judging. What happened, happened.

Another way is for everyone to tell and draw a line describing their emotion during the time frame.

Summary

In this chapter we talked about roles. Kanban is not prescribing any roles; on the contrary, it is telling you to initially not change any of your roles. The roles we have suggested are just roles we have seen improving the system in other places.

Examples of roles we talked about are Kanban Master, who is the master of the process and acts as a shield for the team; and the Product Owner, who prioritizes the backlog and communicates with the stakeholders.

We have also suggested a couple of meetings you could pick from to improve your system. The most important one is the Retrospective meeting since that's the meeting focus on how to improve the process. In the next chapter, it's finally time to start using Kanban for real. You will get an impression of how the first day's schedule could look.

> 6

Day 15 – First Day Running Kanban

You are now ready for your first day of using Kanban. You have spent two weeks in preparation and now it's time to get started.

We will guide you through the day, hour by hour. Please remember that this is just a suggestion of how we would do it in a generic company. As you are probably not working at a generic company, it would probably not fit you perfectly. Instead of following this chapter precisely, see it as an inspiration and use the part that you see could be useful for you.

9:00 to 11:00 – first planning meeting

Gather the people that will be part of this system or process pipeline, that is, the people that will be sharing the same Kanban board.

One person, temporarily or permanently, takes the role as product champion. He or she starts by informing others of the vision for the product or service. He or she continues by showing the roadmap, how to get to the vision, and what the first goal is. The next step in this session is to show the top of the backlog and, if needed, estimate the cases. We don't want extra bureaucracy, so only waste time on estimation if it's absolutely needed.

11:00 to 13:00 – creating your Kanban board

The next part of this day is dedicated to creating your board. We suggest that one person briefs the others about the outcome of the sessions described in *Chapter 2, Days 3-5 – Getting to Know Yyour System*, where you got a better understanding of your system. Inform your team members about the details of your customers and what value you bring to them. Also show the value stream map and the suggestion for the first Kanban board and all the other visualization dimensions.

So far, this may sound very top driven and commanding, and not the broad deciding-things-together strategy that is more associated with Agile methods. Our hope is that most of the people at the meeting have been involved in preparations and that very little is new to them. Anyhow, it's good to summarize and to be clear about the starting point. From now on, everybody will be part of improving the process and introducing the changes needed.

The next step is to create the board together and make sure everyone understands how it works. You can make sure everyone understands what every process step means by writing down a definition of done for each step. A **definition of done** is a policy clarifying what is expected to have been done with a work task before it is allowed to leave a process step. You can also or instead have a **definition of ready** to clarify what is expected to have been done before a task is allowed to enter a process step.

When you have your board, you should fill it with the current work. Help each other to remember what is going on. There should be a place for everything that takes your time. It's better to get it all up now and then decide what should be there and what should not be there. Meetings that are part of your process do not need to be on the board since they are implied. Meetings for planning a later coming project or initiative will probably be useful to have on the board. It's likely that this session forces you to change the structure of the board. At the end of this part, go back to the exercises you did during *Chapter 4, Days 10-11 – Setting the Limits*, and set the limits. By doing this after you have put your work on your board, it's easy to see whether the limits are realistic or not.

You also need to decide the visualization dimensions for the information that is not on the board and not part of the note representing the work. An example is how to signal that a work task is stopped for some reason. The most common solution is to put a red or pink note on the work note to show that the task is stopped. Here is some information you can add to the note:

➤ The reason why it's stopped

➤ Who or what it's waiting for

➤ How long it's been waiting

The next step is to mark the working notes with who is working on it. We recommend you use avatars on magnets for this. You can ask everyone involved to write his or her name and also add a nice picture or just choose a cartoon to represent themselves. Here are two sites where they can get help creating their avatars:

➤ `http://www.faceyourmanga.com/`

➤ `http://southpark.cc.com/avatar`

These sites are almost too good to be true, so check that they still exist and are working before you send out the links.

Don't forget to take a break for lunch during this session. Maybe you can eat together and socialize about other things than your Kanban process.

13:00 to 14:00 – deciding your meetings

Before we are done, we need to decide which meetings we want to have and how often and when to have them. Go back to *Chapter 5, Day 12 – Choosing the Roles and Meetings You Need*, and present the options. Also ask the others for more alternatives. Maybe someone might have some good ideas they have experienced at another company or department. Remember, the idea of Kanban is for you to have an adaptive process where you are encouraged to experiment to prove or discard a hypothesis. So add a meeting if you think it will add value and remove it if you think it won't.

We'd just like to add that there is something strange about communication. When it works, no one thinks it's needed, but when you find out that it doesn't work, it's too late. You should rather have many short meetings than a few long ones. Invite people that are needed when they are needed and not otherwise.

14:00 to 17:00 – start working

Now, when you have planned your near future, decided your initial process, and visualized your current status, it's time to get started doing some actual work. It could be good to start with a daily sync just to make everyone feel they have started and know what they should start doing. This should be obvious with a good Kanban board, but in the beginning it's good to be extra clear, especially if people are used to getting commands on what to do.

While most people start with their ordinary work, some people, for instance the Kanban master if you have one, print the definition of done for each process step, cut them as small as possible, and put each of them with the respective process step on the Kanban board.

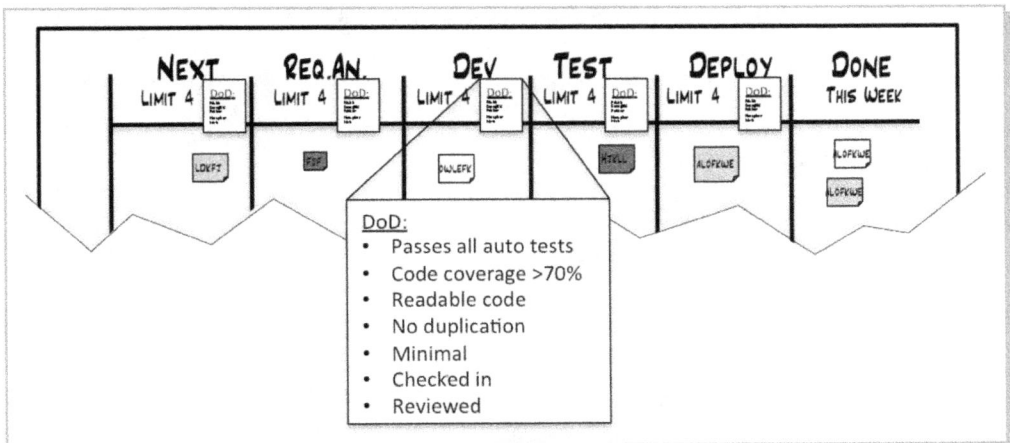

Printed "definition of done" for each column

Someone, maybe the same person, collects the avatars and prints them. To make them last longer, we suggest that you laminate them before gluing them with double-sided tape to a magnet.

A few days later – the first retrospective

When your Kanban implementation is young, a lot of things may go wrong. For that reason, it's good to have a short feedback loop in the beginning. That's why we recommend you have a short retrospective early, maybe even the second or third day. In this situation, we think the plus-minus-delta retrospective is most appropriate. Get the list of the most prioritized changes that are requested. Some of them are probably easy to fix. We usually call them *Just do it*. In this category, there are things like moving the daily sync to another time or to another room. All these changes need is a decision.

For the harder ones that need some effort, you need to have appointed persons and also some way to make sure they will be followed up. That is typically work for a Kanban master, if you have one, or you can handle it together by using a part of your board for improvement work.

While talking about reserved spaces on the board, here is a list of other things that could be useful to have on the board:

➤ Schedule for when people are away for half a day or more

➤ Release schedule

➤ Test environments—which environment to use for what

➤ Branches—which branch to use for what

➤ A list of things to bring up at the next sync meeting

➤ Architecture drawings

Summary

In this chapter, we have given you a suggestion for how to perform on your first day of Kanban implementation. It included:

➤ Planning

➤ Creating your Kanban board

➤ Deciding your meetings

➤ Your very first retrospective

In the next chapter, you will learn how to continuously improve your process and product by verifying hypotheses.

>7

Days 16-29 – Improving Your Process

Yesterday, you started applying Kanban to your process. That means you have agreed to pursue evolutionary change and you are encouraging acts of leadership at all levels. Today is the day to start changing, not just because you should change, but because you and your organization see the benefit of changing. To get inspiration for what to change, we will continue the value stream map, find ways to measure our performance, and look for different kinds of demand. It might be hard to know in advance what changes are good and which are not. To help us figure this out, we take help from Edward Deming and his PDCA.

Edward Deming and PDCA

Edward Deming (1900-1993) was an American professor of statistics at New York University's graduate school of business administration. He's known for his fourteen key principles of business effectiveness. The principles are close to the Lean principles. His most famous contribution is the iterative four-step management method, called **PDCA**, which is used to continuously improve processes and products.

PDCA is short for **Plan-Do-Check-Act**. It starts with a hypothesis, a guess that you want to verify. Then follows the following four steps:

1. In the first step, the planning step, you decide how to do the change and how to know whether it was successful or not.

2. The **Do** step is where you are putting your change into action.

3. In the **Check** step, you look at the criteria you decided in the planning step, typically some sort of measurement, and you decide whether it was a success or a failure.

4. The fourth step is where you act on the result and develop a new hypothesis that you want to verify. You then go back to the first step again.

This loop continues until you decide that a new area needs to be improved. When implementing Kanban, you have agreed to continuously change forever.

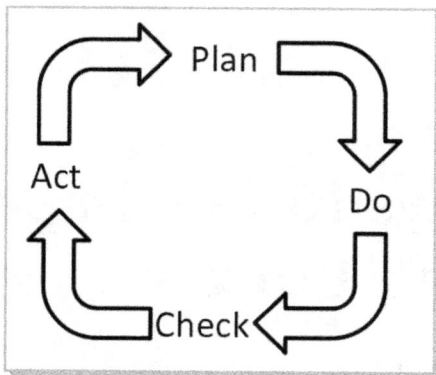

PDCA, an iterative four-step management method to continuously improve processes and products

Changes can be suggested daily during a retrospective or through an extra initiative, for example a task force. It helps a lot if everyone has agreed to test the hypothesis and that everyone involved gets access to the result. It´s great if everyone also participates in the decision to make the change stick, try something else, or go back to the original way of working. To know whether a change is positive or not, there is a need for measurement. A typical Kanban way is to decide the measurement first and to plan the improvement later. That makes it easier to follow up the metrics after the change has been implemented and distinguish success from failure. By continuously updating and clearly announcing metrics, it's easier to align the organization toward the goal.

Measurements to differentiate between improvements from impairments

At the check phase in the PDCA cycle, you check whether your changes improved your measurements. If they improved, continue doing it, if not, reverse and go back or tweak. Together with a change there might be a temporary dip caused by confusion, frustration, or resistance about the change. If you really believe in the change, give it some time before you judge it.

The problem is to measure the right things since what is good from one point of view could cause damage for another view. Here comes some inspiration of what to measure.

Value, failure, and false demand

When people talk about increasing the capacity of the development unit, they usually think of hiring new people or asking people to work overtime or be more efficient. What is often overlooked is whether the developers are working with the right stuff. And this is usually one of the biggest areas of improvement. You can get an understanding of how much improvement you can get by dividing the work into three categories:

> ➤ Category 1 is **value demand**, which is the work that actually brings value to your customers.

> ➤ Category 2 is **failure demand**, which is the work that needs to be redone because it didn't match what the customer expected or it didn't give the expected value. Fixing defects is typically a failure demand. Another kind of failure demand is work that is only there because of earlier failures. An example is meetings to prioritize defects. If you had no defects from the beginning or fixed them immediately when they were found, the meeting was not needed.

> ➤ Category 3 is **false demand**, which is the demand that shouldn't be done. You start to work with it but will never see the value of the time spent. It may be because the work didn't have enough value to pass the system. Instead it was down prioritized and thrown away before it was delivered.

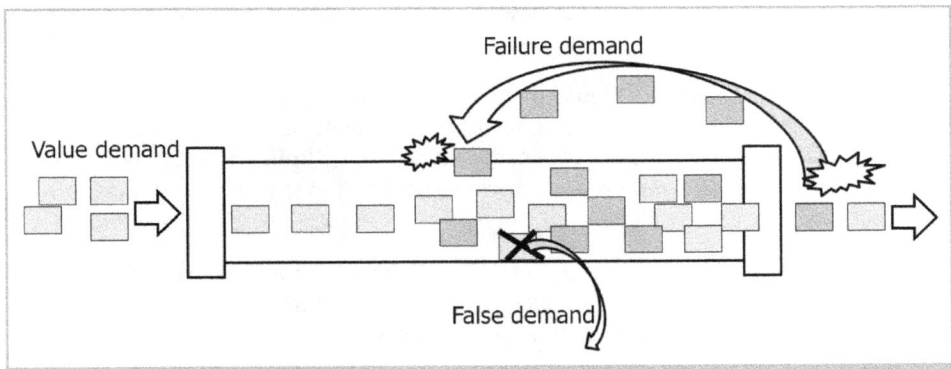

The picture shows the good "value demand" and the time wasting "failure demand" and "false demand"

The goal is obviously to have 100 percent value demand and nothing else. The truth is usually far from that. The big problem with failure and false demand is not the time it takes, it's more the energy it takes from people involved. Very few get energized by fixing defects or by throwing away half-done work. Failure demands also cause turbulence in the flow since they are interrupting the planned work.

Measuring time to market

Another measurement is time to market or lead-time. In this quickly changing world, a late delivery may cause lower earnings. Customers change their minds and competitors are releasing before you do.

By setting a timestamp on your work when you start and another timestamp when you're done, you get a measurement.

It is also valuable to measure the time from when a need is communicated by the customer to when the need is fulfilled. That is an important measurement when you want to know whether you have the right amount of people or not.

Using the right measurements, the right way

Whatever you measure, don't forget to check whether the customers are satisfied with your product or service as well. Adding customer satisfaction, sales figures, returning customers, and net promoter score makes the picture of your performance more complete.

If you use too few measurements, there is a risk of sub-optimization. Alone, most measurements can be manipulated. Let's say you only measure time to market. The behavior you might get if you only focus on that is that all working tasks will be closed immediately without making sure they are fully done. This looks fine, but will it give you happy customers? Probably not.

The behaviors that are really important are usually hard to measure, and what is easy to measure is not always helping you become successful. Or as Russell Ackoff so well put it, "Managers who can't measure what they want, frequently settle for wanting what they can measure."

A good measurement portfolio should include some sort of performance matrix. The problem with performance matrices is that they could easily be manipulated if they stand alone. By measuring lines of code produced, you get code duplication. By measuring velocity (how much a team can produce during a certain time) you get inflation in size, more defects, or ugly code.

There is also a risk of measuring too much. Measurements should take minimal time and energy. Reporting on instances might take little time to do, but since most people don't like it, it drains energy, which reduces the performance.

Continuing your value stream mapping

In *Chapter 2, Days 3-5 – Getting to Know Your System*, you started a value stream map by doing exercise one and two, so now it´s time for step three. Back then, you needed a value stream map to understand your process. Now it's time to complete the map, and it will become a great tool to see problems in your flow and opportunities for improvements.

Exercise III – handling special tracks

In *Chapter 2, Days 3-5 – Getting to Know Your System*, you ended up with a nice flow where all the work flowed downstream all the time. Unfortunately, the reality doesn't usually look like that. Work also needs to go upstream at times, because things need to be redone. It could be defects found or work that becomes much more expensive than estimated. There can also be work that could skip some steps because they are of different size or type. The priority should still be the same as for all of the other items in the workshop. If you see a value in drawing a map for high prioritized work, that's fine, but don't mix them.

Looking for loops and alternate ways

The work tasks are not always passing each of the stations in your system from start to end in the right order. Sometimes work needs to go back because you need to redo something. Other times, work may bypass a station just because the work performed at that station is not applicable for this task. To improve your value stream map, you need to take those special treatments into account. You do it like this:

> ➤ If requests are sent back to an earlier station, then you have a loop. Draw this as an arrow back.

> ➤ If a request needs some special treatment, draw this as a parallel track.

> ➤ Sometimes a loop is better drawn as a parallel track, typically when the steps after an arrow back differ from the normal path. Let's say that, in the following example, the loop from Test back to **change control board** (CCB) is used when testers find changes in existing functionality that needs to be acknowledged by CCB. If the process then is to bypass all the steps between CCB and Test, then this is better done with a parallel track where CCB is mentioned again, instead of a loop back.

In this example, the request to CCB needs to continue the normal path after CCB:

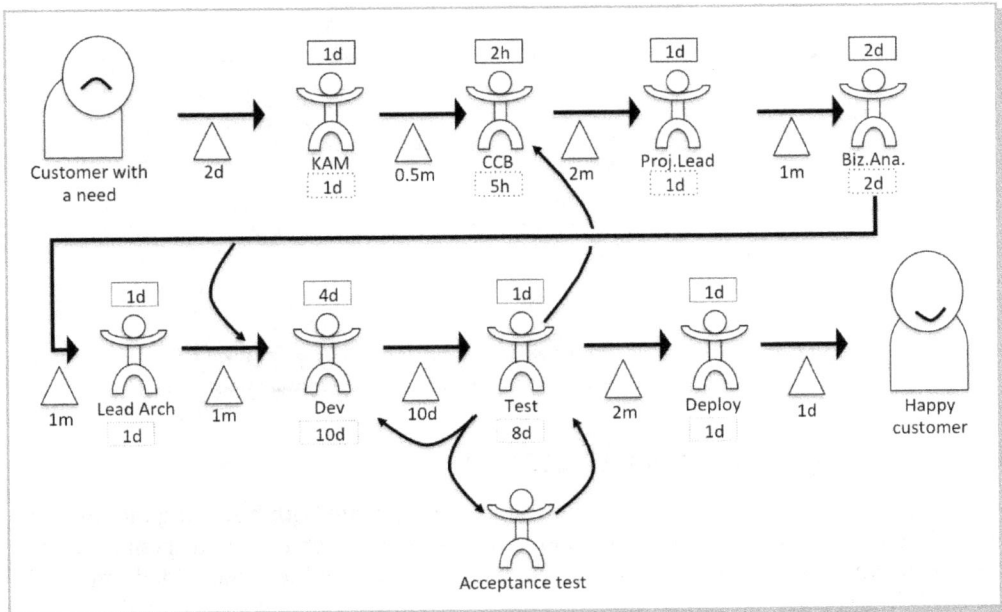

A value stream map including loops and special tracks

Finding the time spent on loops and alternate ways

When you know your alternative paths, you need to know how much time they add or subtract from the total time. This is how you do it:

1. Write what percentage of work tasks go through the special track or go back in the loop.

2. Write the time the loop or extra track takes. Unless some of the work is adding value, it's all written under the symbols. The time of added value is written above:

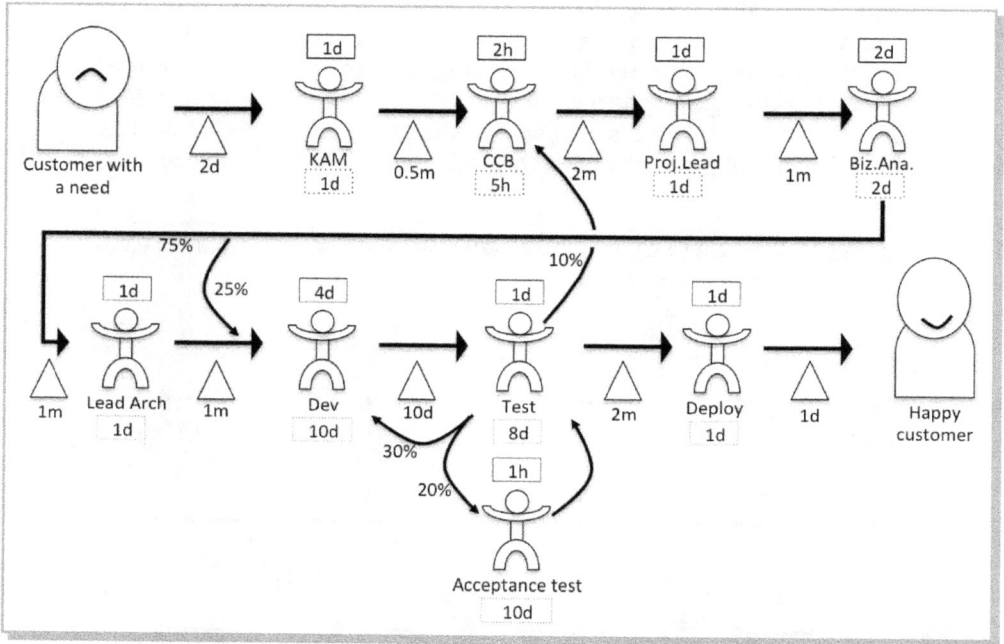

A value stream map with time consumed in loops and special tracks

Calculating process efficiency

When you have the time each station adds, you can calculate both how long the time the normal item takes from idea to deployment and also how much time you spent on that item. You can also calculate the process efficiency by dividing the value added time with the total time spent.

You calculate total time by adding the time under the symbols. The loops makes it a little bit more complicated but it becomes easy if you think of them as separate tracks.

Keep in mind that the figures should be for one item. If you spend 8 days testing 8 items, the time for testing one item is 1 day.

You need to normalize to get a figure you can compare. In this example, our recommendation is to convert all figures to days according to these formulas:

> ➤ 8 hours = 1 day (1d)
> ➤ 1 week = 5 days
> ➤ 1 month = 22 days (working days)
> ➤ 1 year = 260 days

By summarizing the normalized figures, the time spent for the different tracks can be calculated:

> ➤ Main track: 2d+1d+0.5m+5h+2m+1d+1m+2d+1m+1d+1m+10d+10d+8d+2m +1d+1d = 203d
> ➤ 10 percent goes back to CCB: 5h+2m+1d+1m+2d+1m+1d+1m+10d+10d+8d = 143d
> ➤ 25 percent skips lead architect: 1m+1d = 23d
> ➤ 30 percent goes back to developers: 10d+10d+8d = 28d
> ➤ 20 percent passes the acceptance test: 10d
> ➤ Total time spent = 203d + 10%*143d - 25%*23d + 30%*28d + 20%*10d = 222d

As you can see, even though most of the tasks use loops, the loops are adding less than 10 percent to the total number. So maybe it's not worth the increased complexity to add the loops.

Calculate value added time by adding the time above the symbols:

> ➤ Main track: 1d+2h+1d+2d+1d+4d+1d+1d = 11d
> ➤ 10 percent goes back to CCB: 2h + 1d + 2d + 1d + 4d +1d = 9d
> ➤ 25 percent skips lead architect: 1d
> ➤ 30 percent goes back to developers: 4d + 1d = 5d
> ➤ 20 percent passes the acceptance test: 1h
> ➤ Total value added time = 11d + 10%*9d - 25%*1d + 30%*5d = 13d

Calculate process efficiency by dividing value added time by total time:

> ➤ 13d / 222d = 6%

This means that in this example, it takes 222 days to get 13 days of work through the system. In other terms, it takes 10 months to implement an idea from a customer. Sounds crazy, but it's not that uncommon!

Finding improvements in the process

In the previous example, we saw that it's theoretically possible to reduce the time to market from 222 days down to 13 days without reducing the quality or any other value adding time.

By understanding this, you have a fantastic source of improvement opportunities.

Here comes some advice of what to look for:

> ➤ Look at the queues, that is, the triangles in front of each station. What's in them? Why are they there, and most importantly, how can they be reduced or even removed? To visualize the content of the queue, you can write the number of items in the queue in the triangle. One of the best pieces of advice we can give you is to improve collaboration between stations or even put them in the same cross-functional team.

> ➤ Reduce the number of stations. Do you need a CCB, a project leader, a business analyst, a lead architect, and a separate person for deploying? A DevOps team (a team handling developing, testing, and deploying) that talks directly with the customer will bypass most of these stations. Even if the cost for developers would increase, the value will probably increase more. Most people like to work end-to-end with higher motivation and productivity as the result, so development cost might even be reduced.

> ➤ Look at the difference in time spent and added value time within a station and figure out the reason for time spent to be higher. Are you working with many things in parallel?

> ➤ Some parts of the queues are there to absorb variation in work size. A common motivation for keeping queues is "We need to have something to do when the others are working on something big." Our advice here is to split work down into smaller-sized chunks of work for all of the people involved. It will give a better flow. Another is to mentally convince people that some time of not knowing what to do, or slack, is good for the flow. The slack time can be used for improvements. Limits is a great way to improve flow, and slack is an obvious time to discuss improvements.

Removing unnecessary queues

There are good and bad queues. Good queues are there to handle variance; that is, leveling workload and improving flow. It could be a few things in a work backlog just to make sure there are things to do even if the product owner is gone for a day or two. Good queues are short and even empty from time to time.

Bad queues are long and never empty. Look at the following two graphs showing the number of tickets in a bug database over time. The waves are symbolizing variation in reporting new tickets (in-flow) and variation in capacity to handle tickets. They both have the capacity needed since the average number of tickets is stable.

They are both showing the same productivity and in-flow over time. That is, the same number of tickets are coming in and the same number of tickets are handled. The difference is the time it takes before a new ticket is handled.

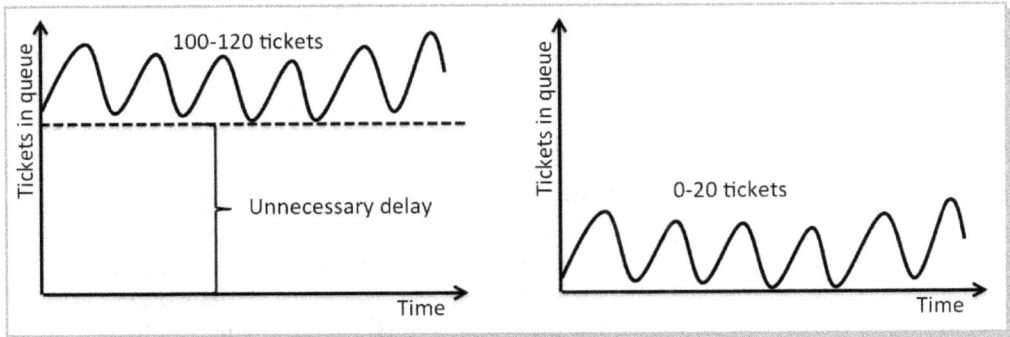

A graph showing two teams with different amounts of defects in their backlog

Let's say that both teams use a first come, first serve algorithm and they both handle on average 10 tickets per week. For the team to the left, this means an average of eleven weeks to deliver, which can be compared to a one-week delivery time for the team to the right. They have the same in-flow and the same capacity, but the left team has a much longer waiting time.

Unnecessary waiting time is not the only problem caused by this queue. The risk of duplicates is much higher when working with a queue with about 110 tickets compared to a queue with only about 10 tickets. There is also a risk that the defect can't easily be reproduced when developers are charged with fixing the defect. It's much easier to fix a defect that has just happened. The point here is that the queue in itself costs time, money, and energy.

The best way to go away from the long queue is to never get there, but if you get there, here are a few ways of removing the queue:

➤ The most radical way is to throw away all old tickets.

➤ Set a policy to handle all tickets immediately or throw them away.

➤ Add extra capacity during a limited time to reduce the tickets to zero.

➤ For teams working with both new development and bug fixing, introduce bug-fixing Mondays, where everyone in the team spend all their time on fixing defects.

Another challenge is to stay at a low level. This can be done by:

➤ Doing any of the things mentioned previously.

➤ Limit the number of incoming tickets per week. When reaching the limit, the input is closed.

> ➤ Limit the number of tickets in the queue. When reaching the limit, every new
> ticket should either be thrown away or replace a ticket already in the queue,
> which will be thrown away.

Some people have a problem throwing away tickets, but adding work to an already
overloaded system will cause decreased capacity, which will only make the situation
even worse.

Prioritizing with algorithms

Most companies have managers to decide what to do and the prioritization of it. But in
many cases, the selection could be done with a simple algorithm instead. The good thing
is that we can reduce the number of managers and also remove one station that causes
time loss. This also means one less person between the customer and the workers, and
every person between the customer and the workers causes some change in the message
of what the customer values. It's like the whispering game kids play. What the customer
asks for may not be the same as what the workers are asked to do. Without manual
prioritization, we need to decide how to prioritize using an algorithm instead.

The algorithm for selecting work in the right order can be something simple like first
come, first serve, or specifically **first in first out** (**FIFO**), which is not considering
anything about value.

Another algorithm is to sort highest value first. If you consider cost as well, you can sort
the tasks by placing the task that produces the highest revenue first.

An even more advanced way is to take time into account and calculate a graph for cost
of delay, that is, how much it will cost to delay work by a day, a week, a month, or a year.
Look at the following graph. It shows cost of delay for two features; one is a cool feature
for a campaign lasting for a month and the second is a window of opportunity that will
last for three months. If both tasks take 1 month to do, which one would you do first?

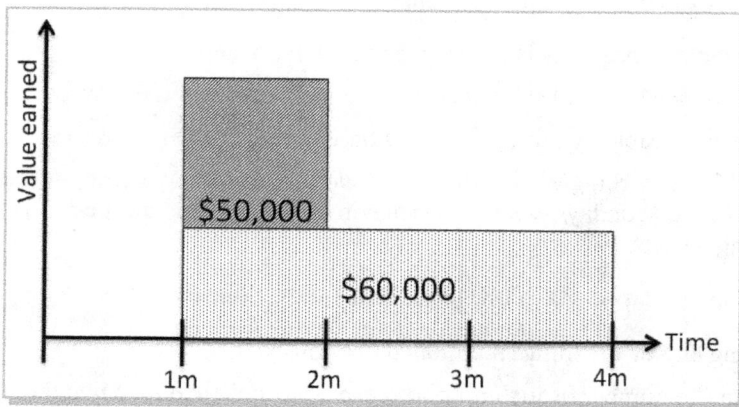

Algorithm showing which task to do first when prioritizing revenue

The correct answer would be to do the $50,000 campaign feature first since the cost of delaying that work will cost you $50,000 per month, while the $60,000 work is only worth $20,000 per month even though the total value is higher.

The next example comes from a company developing business systems and a team working with maintenance. Before they implemented Kanban, they worked with many things at the same time. This was caused by the friendly attitude to start something as soon as someone shouted loud enough about it. By implementing Kanban, they limited the number of things they worked on at the same time, but still it didn't work very well since they spent a lot of time arguing with stakeholders about what to take next and explaining why issues were waiting so long without getting started.

A quick analysis showed that there were six stakeholders representing different areas of the world. Their view of the maintenance department was a black hole in which they just dumped work without getting much out of it.

A good principle for getting a nice flow is to push work back to the customer, out of the system, and follow the mantra to stop starting and instead start finishing. They achieved this by giving each market representative the control of their own queue as long as no work was put on the issue from the maintenance team. This person didn't need to contact the maintenance people to change their own priority; he or she just changed it according to what was most important at the moment. No shouting to get things prioritized. Just put the most important thing first in line.

To prioritize between the stakeholders, the department used a simple round robin algorithm. That means they took turns without putting any time on trying to figure out which of the stakeholders had the most need. The way of prioritizing is described in the following figure:

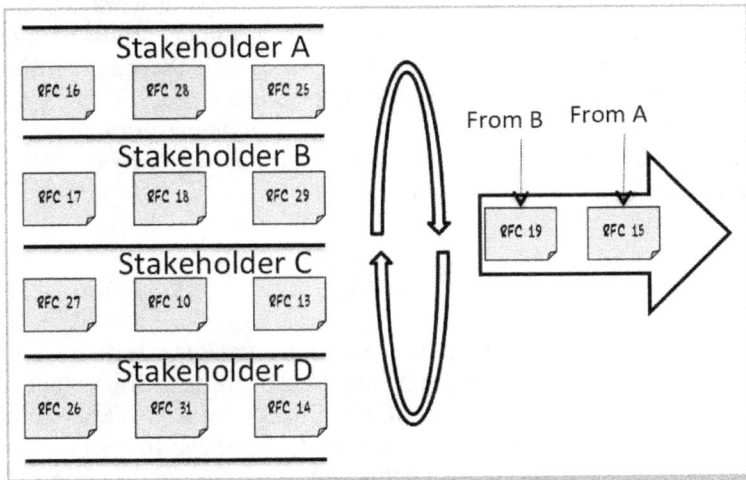

Round robin is a way of serializing a parallel flow of issues

The stakeholders had total control over their queue and the maintenance department was focused on passing as much as possible through their system. This simple thing gave a fantastic result. The time to get things done was almost immediately reduced by 30 percent.

However, when you set up your prioritization, there is always a risk of someone trying to manipulate the process for their own advantage. In the example with round robin, there is a risk of one stakeholder bundling work in one ticket to get more time from the maintenance department. The weakness with round robin is that how much work is spent on the ticket is not taken into consideration. Big things get the same value and cost as a small thing.

One way to level out this unfairness and stop the risk of inflation of ticket sizes is to measure the total time spent per stakeholder. You then know how much time each stakeholder has gotten from you. If there is a need for compensating some of them, from time to time, you can override the round robin algorithm and take two issues from a stakeholder you have spent less time on.

Prioritizing with severity

Another way of prioritizing is to let the stakeholders categorize their tickets. You may then have some simple policies to run your system. Just by adding some simple rules you can get a self-organizing system where everybody knows what they should do, not because someone tells them, but because they know.

To give an example, let's say we have three levels of severity: normal, hot, and super-hot. Normal might be new features and change requests to the product you are working on while hot are important defects and super-hot are critical issues we need to take care of immediately. We have a principle saying that we should drop our work and take care of the issue if it's classified as super-hot. If it's just hot we should continue with our work but as soon as someone is done he or she should take this next. If there are neither hot nor super-hot then we work with the normal issues in prioritized order. This is an example of how a simple principle steers the process and provides guidelines for in which order any issues should be dealt with. This helps to ensure that if anything new or unexpected crops up, the wider process is not negatively affected.

Summary

In this chapter, we covered the idea of continuous improvement by verifying hypotheses. You know hypotheses that are right and that are wrong by using measurement. We call this infinite loop PDCA because of its parts: Plan, Do, Check, and Act. We have completed our value stream map and calculated the process efficiency. You have also got tips about how to remove unnecessary queues and prioritize with algorithms.

In the next chapter, we will see how to plan future deliveries when your work is hard to predict.

> 8

Day 30 – Release Planning

You should by now have been running a Kanban system for two weeks and we hope you have seen some improvements and got some measurements in place. It's now time to try and predict the future, that is, what to release and when. First we want to set your expectations correct; there are no ways to get forecasting correct for sure.

"Prediction is very difficult. Especially about the future"

- Niels Bohr

Since it's so hard to predict the future, instead of putting a lot of effort in planning, we choose a way of working that gives us early warnings if and when plans go wrong. That gives us a possibility to react in time if needed.

Our recommendation is to have the following three things in mind when you decide your planning method:

1. Base your planning on observed facts instead of advanced guessing. That means basing your plans on historic facts and interpolating future expectations. As time passes you learn more so update your plan continuously as your knowledge increases.

2. Put minimum time on planning because the customers will not pay for the time you spend on it. Plan just enough so you are able to handle dependency on others within the same project or on people preparing future projects. Planning is also important while deciding whether to stop, cut, or continue a project. Everything besides what is absolutely necessary is waste.

3. Plan in the way you get minimum risk if your plan is wrong.

Basing your plan on facts

To be able to base your plan on facts, the first thing is to collect facts. This is the reason why this topic is brought up as late as in the last chapter. If you followed the schedule in this book you should by now have metrics from 2 weeks of work, where you know how many items you can handle during two weeks, the average time to market, and the average time spent on an item. This is important information when trying to predict the future.

When looking at the facts you have you will see variation in both size of work and in how much time was spent working on your items during a day. Some days are focused with little interruptions while other days are spent in meetings and on unpredicted things.

To reduce the variation you need to take control over the amount of work and make sure you get your workdays more leveled out.

Taking control over the amount of work

There are two ways of getting control over the amount of work. One way is to break things down in equal sizes. Big things are broken down and small things are put together. If they are really small just do them instead of putting time on putting them together. The other way to get control of the amount of work is to estimate. Estimating does not change the variation of size but it helps you get control over variation on the difference between estimated volume and real volume.

It's important to remember that there is no science in estimating and there is no way to get it perfect so don't look for perfection and don't connect estimation with incentives or commitment. It will only lead to problems in the form of vagueness, bad quality due to shortcuts taken to meet a deadline, and unreasonable high estimates with low engagement energy from the team.

There are though some ways to improve your estimates:

1. The people that will do the work should do the estimations. They would know best how much work is needed.

2. Don't estimate in hours; use relative estimations instead. It's much easier and becomes more accurate to tell which task will be more complex when comparing two, instead of guessing how many days and hours they will take. If you are doing the same things over and over again it might be easier to estimate in time, but for the development of new features, comparing one task with another is easier. Don't worry, as you can get plans in days even without time estimates on the work (see Knowing your capacity and calculating delivery date in the following section).

You should not spend more time on estimating than is absolutely necessary. We have never seen a project fail because of bad estimation. We have seen projects fail but then it's because of unknown things, things that were not predicted from the beginning or just simply because of bad communication.

Quick estimating

Quick estimating is done during a 1-2 hours workshop and goes like this:

1. Gather all the people working on a project around a table.

2. At the center of the table, place one note for each task involved in the project.

3. The facilitator asks the people gathered if all the tasks are of the same size. (Here, size refers to the amount of work needed to complete the task). If so, the discussion can end, but in normal cases the answer is "no".

4. The facilitator will then ask the people to move tasks that are substantially bigger than the other tasks to one side of the table and what is substantially smaller to the other side of the table. The work that is about average should remain in the middle. It's important to have someone available who can answer questions about what the work is about.

5. You should now have three bunches of work, one for small items, one for medium items, and one for large items. The facilitator will now ask again whether the items in each bunch are of equal size. If the answer is no, the bunches of items can be divided in three. That means that the medium becomes medium small, medium medium, and medium large.

6. You should now have your items divided in three or nine sizes, but to be able to plan you need to give the groups' figures that could be compared on the same scale. We suggest you use the modified Fibonacci scale for this. If you have nine bunches the scale means 1, 2, and 3 for the small, 5, 8, and 13 for the medium and 20, 40, and 100 for the large.

If the preceding answer at step 5 is yes, then you can use 2 for small, 8 for medium, and 40 for large. This means the size of one medium is the same as the sum of 4 small. The same goes for the difference between medium and large. The following diagram illustrates the process.

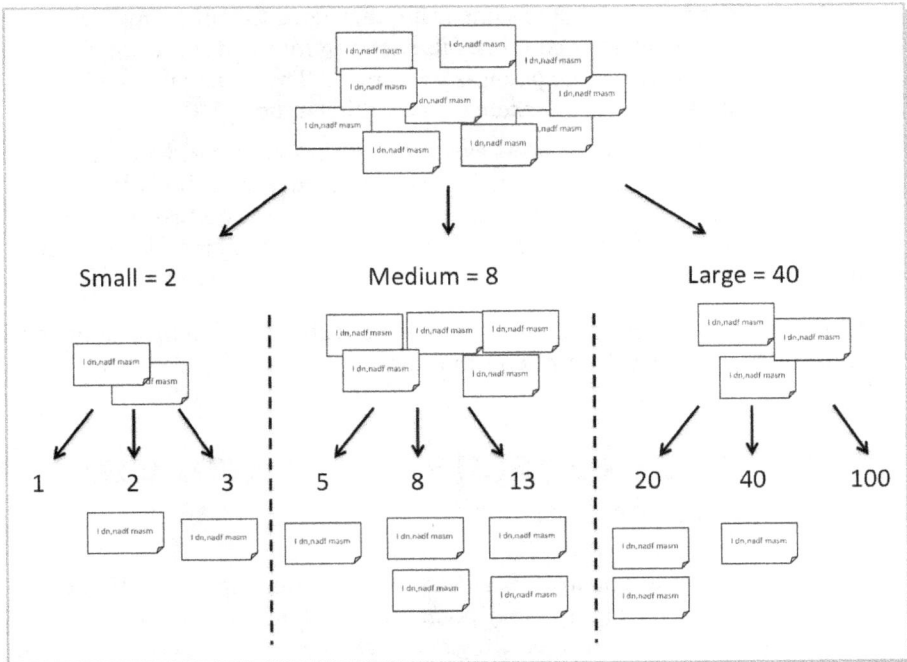

Quick estimating is done by dividing your work in three bunches and later in nine bunches, if needed

The figures don't say anything about how long, in hours or days, it will take to complete the work. It's just a unit telling the relative difference in size. A common name for this unit is **story points** since items often are called stories or user stories. The correct definition for a user story is out of the scope of this book, but if you want to know more search for "agile user story Mike Cohn" on the Internet.

Estimating with the planning poker

Planning poker is an estimation method introduced by Mike Cohn. This is how it works:

1. The people that will do the work are gathered and each of them get a deck of cards with values: 0, 1/2 , 1, 2, 3, 5, 8, 13, 20, 40, and 100. A person with knowledge about a feature that will be developed, typically a business analyst or a product owner, presents it to the people who will work with it and asks them to estimate the effort of work needed to complete the feature. The estimation should be relative to some other features the people involved have already worked with. If the reference feature had the size 8 and the new feature is almost twice as big, the estimator should pick the card with 13 written on it.

2. The estimators get time to ask a lot of questions before they are able to give an estimate.

3. When the questions are answered it's time for everyone to choose a card that represents their estimation.

4. When all the estimators have selected a card, they simultaneously show their cards.

5. If they are not all showing the same result they need to argue why they chose the card. Some of the reasons could be false assumptions and some could be things not even the knowledgeable one was thinking of. This is actually the biggest advantage of planning poker exercises according to us.

6. After new questions and answers everybody picks new cards, which are shown with the new debate as the result. This continues until everybody is showing the same card. If it's just impossible to get an end of the discussions, go for the highest estimation, so no one can say they got pushed to give a lower estimation than they wanted.

We recommend you use quick estimation when you are at the beginning of a project and planning poker when you have a few items to estimate.

Knowing your capacity and calculating the delivery date

Now, when you know the size of work you need to know your capacity. The **capacity**, also known as **velocity**, is how many story points your system can complete during a certain time period, for instance a week. To get the velocity you also need to estimate the work you completed during the last weeks.

With both, the total size of a project and a velocity, you can calculate how long the project will take to complete.

Let's say the sum of all the work in the project is estimated to 200 story points and your capacity is 20 story points per week. Easy math will tell you that the project will take 10 weeks to complete. The result has more value than the traditional way of guessing before the project has started. It's based on real facts and if people are always too optimistic when estimating it will be reflected in the velocity so the calculation will be correct anyway.

The most important thing is not to have an estimated release date, especially since it's based on early guessing. It's more important to continuously follow-up and early get a warning that the plan needs adjustments. This can be done with a burn down graph.

Follow-up progress with a burn-down chart

A burn down graph is a simple tool to follow up your progress:

1. Start with an empty graph. On the y axis you put a scale for story points where your total amount of story points for the project is 90 percent up.

2. Put a dot at the level of your total sum of story points. The reason for not putting the total on the top is because it's normal to discover more work that was not found in advance and there needs to be room for that.

3. On the *x* axis you put a scale where the calculated delivery date is about 80 percent away.

4. Put a dot at the targeted delivery date.

5. Draw a dotted line between the two dots. This is the ideal line and will help us see deviation from plan.

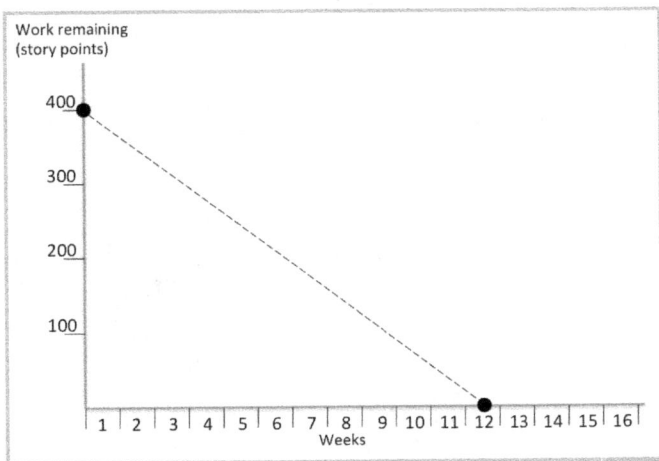

A burn down graph with a dotted line between the starting number of story points in the project and the date when the work is expected to be done

If you're used to GANTT diagrams, you may miss the connection between work and people. That's the whole idea; it's up to the people who do the work to decide and they should make the decisions as late as possible, just in time, when they need to decide. That's when they know who is best suited to do it, considering:

➤ Who has time available.

➤ Who has the correct knowledge.

➤ Who needs to learn to spread the knowledge. This is to reduce the risk of only having one person with some knowledge.

Now you have a plan but a plan is like a weather forecast. Of course the weather forecasters want the 10 day weather forecast to be true, but when they no longer believe in it they need to update the forecast. It's the same with a plan. When you no longer believe in it you need to re-plan and communicate the new forecast. If you are receiving forecast updates, which you are not very fond of, think of it as weather changes. If the rain is coming, the rain is coming, and there's nothing you can do about it. Just hearing the weather presenters talking about sunshine will not help.

The next step is to follow-up your progress. After each week you insert a new dot depending on how much work there is still to do. Work is expected to grow, shrink, be added, be removed or even replaced with something else, all according to the Lean ideas of making decisions late. So don't panic if your line is not following the dotted line. There is no value in trying to follow the doted line. It's like holding an umbrella over the rain gauge just because the weather forecast said it would not rain. The graph is there just to give you an idea of the status and to get it early.

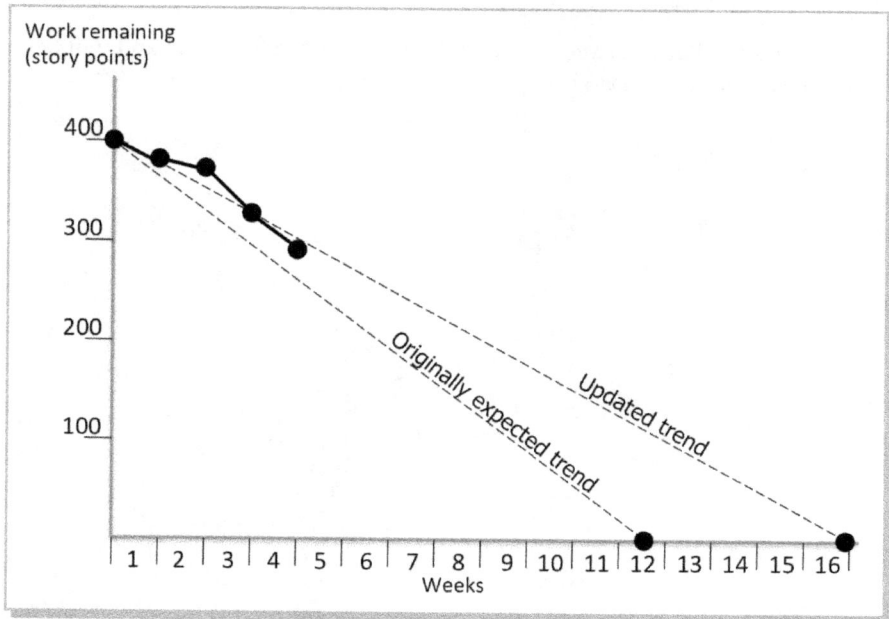

A burn down graph with an updated trend line based on the result from the first five weeks

We have discovered that information is something you deserve and can't be taken for granted. If you feel uninformed it might be because you have reacted in an unpleasant way earlier when you got "bad news". Think of it as if there is no such thing as good or bad news, it' just news, and the earlier you get it the better it is.

If you get bad news early there is still time to react, which is of course better than to get late surprises.

Here are some ways you can act if your burn down graph is showing delays:

> **Cut the scope**: Remove the work with least value and save that for a later release.

> **Add more people**: This does not always work since more people also mean more communication and more knowledge spreading. It's not uncommon that adding people actually delays the release even more because of these factors and the confusion and misunderstandings that come with it.

> **Accept the delay**: The risk here is to grow a never-mind-culture and continuous delays may cause distrust from stakeholders.

Of these three the first, cut the scope, is the one we recommend since it's best for fast feedback and **return of investment** (**ROI**).

There is a forth alternative, which is to take short cuts. We are definitely not recommending this if the work is part of a product that will live more than a few weeks. It's against Lean's first principle about long-term thinking and is, according to us, the most common reason for later problems with development productivity. Unfortunately, this is a very common choice since this is what will happen if none of the preceding three alternatives are successful. It's sometimes badly disguised in terms such as deadline, commitment, take responsibility, and working overtime, but the result is the same—bad quality.

The forth value of the Agile manifesto says that we (the authors of the manifesto) value responding to change over following a plan. That means that the importance is not to get the plan perfect from the beginning but how you react when reality shows that the plan is no longer correct. Our interpretation is that we should spend minimum effort on planning (but not less then that) and more effort on following up and reacting in good ways. Just doing the planning, however, has value since it helps the teams to understand the work. Dwight D. Eisenhower aptly said: "In preparing for battle, I have always found that plans are useless but planning is indispensable."

Communicating the plan

It's also important to separate the plan and communicated message. The plan should be without buffers but the message communicated should have buffers depending on the punishment of divergence from the plan. If the punishment is huge the buffer should also be huge, but if the punishment is close to none, the buffer could be the real estimation.

The reason for separating internal plans and status updates from what is externally communicated is because plans, which include buffers, seem to result in low energy in the team. There is even a law articulated for this. It's called Parkinson's law and goes like this: "work expands so as to fill the time available for its completion". That means that if we include buffers in our plan, the buffers will be used.

In cases where the scope may vary, you can decide how much to communicate. Let's say the marketing department needs to know what will be delivered so they can start producing a future campaign. Then it's good risk handling to ask them to communicate features in the top section of the prioritized list, since they are very likely to be developed. The good news is that's where the most valuable features are and as long as you develop in the same order, starting with the most valuable things, you can be pretty sure the marketing campaign will be correct.

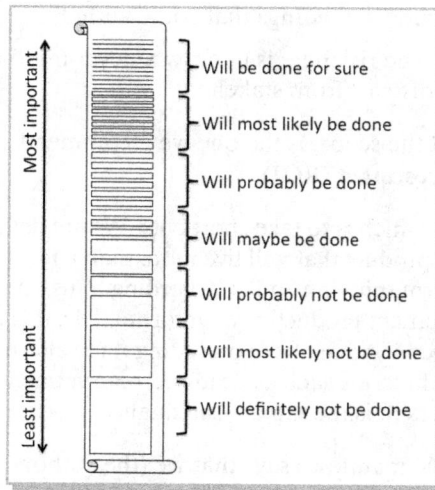

A list of work prioritized in order of importance.

As you can see in the preceding diagram, the top items are thin, concrete, and well defined while the things at the bottom are big and fluffy. That's what we try to illustrate anyway. The reason for working in this way is to minimize wastage, since low prioritized work is not very likely to be done anyway. Time spent on preparing work that might not be done is waste.

Burn-up graph

The close cousin to the burn down graph is the burn up graph. While the burn down graph shows how much there is left, the burn up graph shows how much that has been done. This is even more flexible and easy to start with since you don't need to estimate the whole project from the beginning. You still need to estimate the work before you start working with just that part. The alternative of estimating after it's done will just be a predictable graph showing the time spent on the project so that is nothing we recommend. If your items are of a similar size there is no need for estimating, just counting is enough.

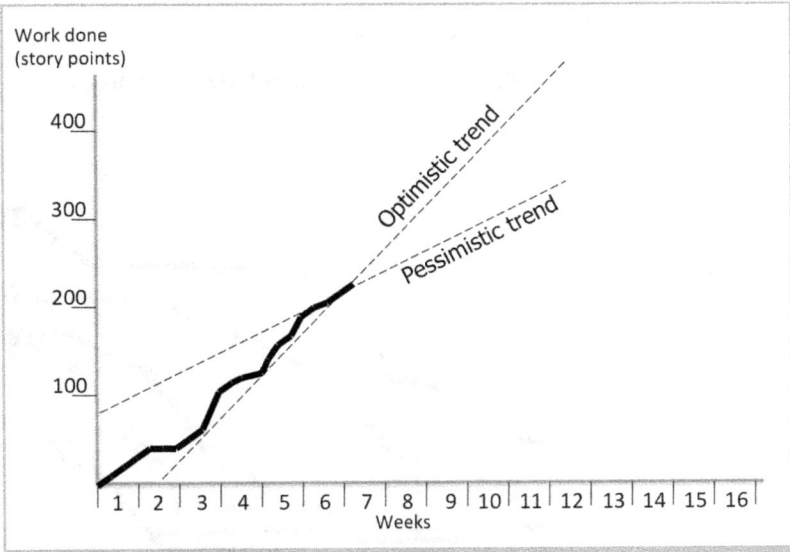

A burn up graph showing the work that has been done together with trend lines showing expected future.

In the preceding burn up graph diagram you see two dashed lines representing the optimistic and the pessimistic trends. The expected outcome will be somewhere in between. From the graph you are able to draw conclusions about when a certain amount of work will be done (the following graph on the left-hand side) or what will be done at a certain date (the following graph on the right-hand side).

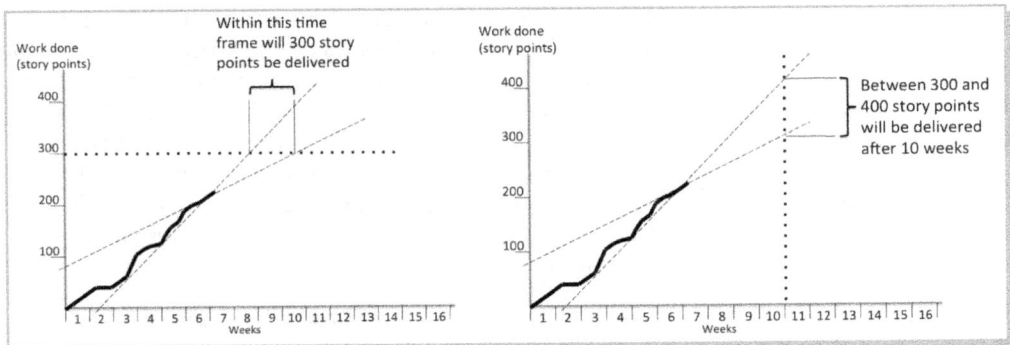

From the burn up graph you can see when something can be expected to be done and about how much that will be done a certain time

Cumulative flow diagram

A common graph used together with Kanban is the cumulative flow diagram. It looks like what is shown in the following diagram:

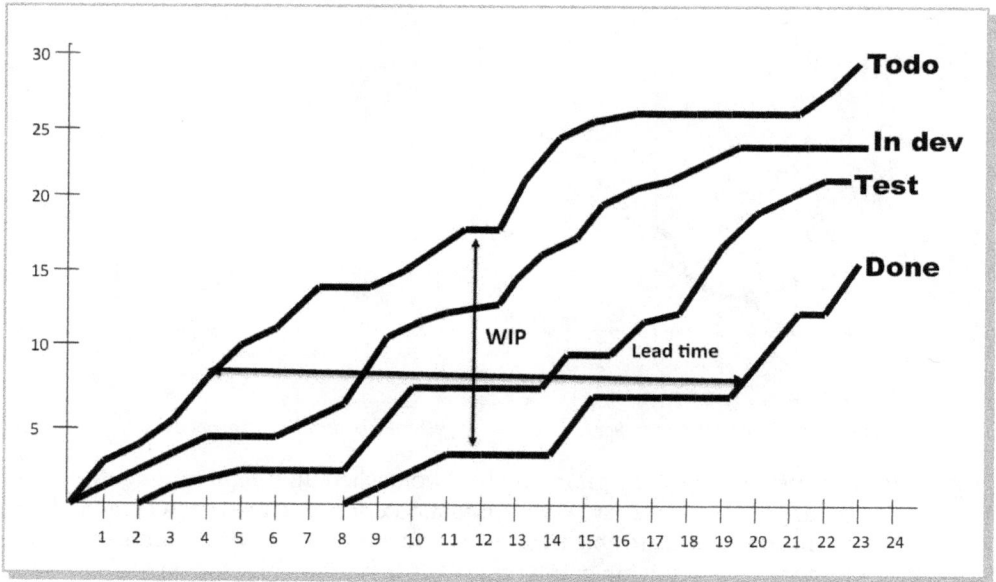

A cumulative flow diagram shows the number of items in each column

The diagram shows the accumulated number of issues in a flow with the four statuses: Todo, In dev, Test, and Done. After one day there are 3 issues on the board, 2 in Todo, and 1 in In dev. On day 9 there is 1 issue Done. That means we have spent 8 days to complete it, which means that is we have a lead-time of 8 days. At the same day there are 13 not done things on the board. The Todo line is on 14 and 1 thing is in Done. This means you can see lead-time as the horizontal difference between the Todo line and the Done line and the WiP as the vertical difference between the same lines. You can see the actual amount a certain date and the trend. If the difference between two lines is increasing you can expect there is a bottleneck in your system.

The advantage of the cumulative flow diagram is that it can be used for many things:

➤ The done line is a burn up and can be used for project planning

➤ The horizontal distance between the lines gives a hint about how good your system is doing

➤ The vertical distance between the lines gives a hint about what is wrong with your system

Taking control over velocity

A graph can never be better than the data it's based on. To be able to trust the burn up/down graph you need to be sure that what is said to be done really is 100 percent done and not just almost done. If work is remaining but hidden your prediction will never be correct. The tool for this is to specify the **definition of done** so that when someone says they are done it's clear for everyone what has been done and what is left to do. The other tool is to have short feedback loops with continuous verification.

It's very hard to predict how much work there will be to correct problems found during a performance test or an acceptance test before you have done the test. The result could be that everything is clear or that you need to redo the whole work. The following graph is a typical symptom of hidden work that is kept to the end of the project:

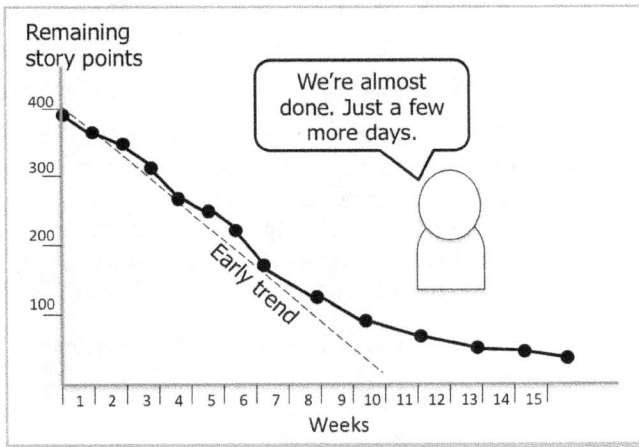

The typical burn down graph for teams that keep testing, documenting, and deploying to the end of the project

With the continuous testing of new functions, old functions, stability, performance, and whatever else you test, you will continuously spend time on fixing the problems found and the risk for late surprises will be reduced. You will also have a status that could be trusted. Even other work that needs to be done before going into production needs to be done continuously. We're thinking of issues such as writing different kinds of documents, fixing the user interface, and training on deploying to a production like environment.

Some situations are very hard to predict the capacity that could be spent on projects. We are mainly thinking of teams that also work with maintenance. A useful tool to get consistent capacity for standard project mix hard-to-predict expedite work with less immediately important work, also known as intangible work.

Intangible work refers to work that is important enough to be done but the cost of waiting is low, at least for the near future. It could be upgrading tools and environment or taking a day for developing new ideas.

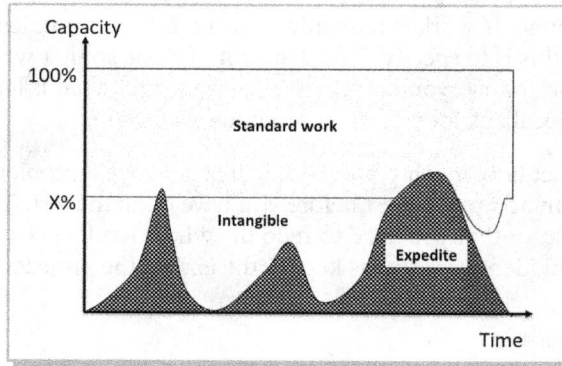

Balance expedite work with intangible work just to get a more constant capacity for standard project work

A real-life story about balancing comes from a company in the finance business. This team was working both with projects, mostly setting up new customers and improving the operation situation, and making sure the service for existing customers was working. Some days they spent most of their time on fire fighting and some days they could spend the whole day on projects. Since the variation in available time was so big, the team didn't want to give the stakeholders any guess for when projects could be done.

The solution was for the team to only plan 50 percent of their time over a two-week period. The prioritization was:

1. Fighting fires.
2. Planned project work.
3. Other work that was needed but not planned.

If they were not able to complete the work for a two-week period the work was hopefully done in the next period together with the work that was planned for those weeks.

This was a simple way of going from unpredictable to predictable.

Summary

In this chapter you learned how to estimate and make a plan out of your estimates. We went through the planning method quick estimating where a whole project could be planned in short time as well as planning poker, which is great for improving an understanding of the work to do.

We told you about three graphs to follow-up the status, including the burn down graph, which was showing the status according to plan; the burn up graph, which showed how much was done and what to expect ahead; and, finally, the cumulative flow diagram, which gave hints about what to expect, how your system is doing, and where the problems are.

We also talked about the importance of observing the progress and reacting rather than forcing the plan. This is to minimize risk for irrational decisions and bad quality, which will cause much bigger problems in the future. Kanban is about a constant or higher pace during a long time.

Congratulations! You are finally at the end of this book. We hope you have a work process that the people involved understand and find easy to follow and an improvement process that helps you continuously improve. We also hope you have a visualization and a plan that support your process and makes people feel comfortable. If you don't feel you're really there yet, no worries, as long as you keep your limits and continuously improve, sooner or later, you will be there. Remember, Kanban is a direction, not a destination. Your Kanban journey will continue forever. Good luck and we wish you a happy journey!

www.ingramcontent.com/pod-product-compliance
Lightning Source LLC
Chambersburg PA
CBHW051226200326
41519CB00025B/7263